JIM THORPE

NORTH AMERICAN INDIANS OF ACHIEVEMENT

JIM THORPE

Sac and Fox Athlete

Bob Bernotas

Senior Consulting Editor

W. David Baird

Howard A. White Professor of History

Pepperdine University

CHELSEA HOUSE PUBLISHERS

New York Philadelphia

FRONTISPIECE   Jim Thorpe, photographed at the 1912 Olympics in Stockholm, Sweden.

ON THE COVER   A portrait of Jim Thorpe in the uniform of the Carlisle Indians, based on a 1910 photograph.

Chelsea House Publishers
EDITOR-IN-CHIEF   Remmel Nunn
MANAGING EDITOR   Karyn Gullen Browne
PICTURE EDITOR   Adrian G. Allen
ART DIRECTOR   Maria Epes
ASSISTANT ART DIRECTOR   Howard Brotman
MANUFACTURING DIRECTOR   Gerald Levine
SYSTEMS MANAGER   Lindsey Ottman
PRODUCTION MANAGER   Joseph Romano
PRODUCTION COORDINATOR   Marie Claire Cebrián

North American Indians of Achievement
SENIOR EDITOR   Liz Sonneborn

Staff for JIM THORPE
ASSOCIATE EDITOR   Philip Koslow
COPY EDITOR   Ian Wilker
EDITORIAL ASSISTANT   Michele Berezansky
DESIGNER   Debora Smith
PICTURE RESEARCHER   Alan Gottlieb
COVER ILLUSTRATION   Bill Donahey

Printed and bound in Mexico.

First Printing

1   3   5   7   9   8   6   4   2

Library of Congress Cataloging-in-Publication Data

Bernotas, Bob.
Jim Thorpe: Sac and Fox athlete/by Bob Bernotas.
    p. cm.—(North American Indians of achievement)
Includes index.
Summary: A biography of the American Indian who won gold medals in the pentathlon and decathlon at the 1912 Olympics and played both professional baseball and football.
ISBN   0-7910-1722-2
1. Thorpe, Jim, 1887–1953—Juvenile literature. 2. Athletes—United States—Biography—Juvenile literature. [1. Thorpe, Jim, 1887–1953. 2. Athletes. 3. Indians of North America—Biography.] I. Title. II. Series.
GV697.T5B47 1992   91-38918
796'.092—dc20   CIP
[B]   AC

CONTENTS

NORTH AMERICAN INDIANS OF ACHIEVEMENT

BLACK HAWK
Sac Rebel

JOSEPH BRANT
Mohawk Chief

COCHISE
Apache Chief

CRAZY HORSE
Sioux War Chief

CHIEF GALL
Sioux War Chief

GERONIMO
Apache Warrior

HIAWATHA
Founder of the Iroquois
Confederacy

CHIEF JOSEPH
Nez Perce Leader

PETER MACDONALD
Former Chairman of the Navajo
Nation

WILMA MANKILLER
Principal Chief of the Cherokees

OSCEOLO
Seminole Rebel

QUANAH PARKER
Comanche Chief

KING PHILIP
Wampanoag Rebel

**POCAHONTAS AND CHIEF
POWHATAN**
Leaders of the Powhatan Tribes

PONTIAC
Ottawa Rebel

RED CLOUD
Sioux War Chief

WILL ROGERS
Cherokee Entertainer

SEQUOYAH
Inventor of the Cherokee Alphabet

SITTING BULL
Chief of the Sioux

TECUMSEH
Shawnee Rebel

JIM THORPE
Sac and Fox Athlete

SARAH WINNEMUCCA
Northern Paiute Writer and
Diplomat

Other titles in preparation

ON INDIAN LEADERSHIP

by W. David Baird

Howard A. White Professor of History
Pepperdine University

Authoritative utterance is in thy mouth, perception is in thy heart, and thy tongue is the shrine of justice," the ancient Egyptians said of their king. From him, the Egyptians expected authority, discretion, and just behavior. Homer's *Iliad* suggests that the Greeks demanded somewhat different qualities from their leaders: justice and judgment, wisdom and counsel, shrewdness and cunning, valor and action. It is not surprising that different people living at different times should seek different qualities from the individuals they looked to for guidance. By and large, a people's requirements for leadership are determined by two factors: their culture and the unique circumstances of the time and place in which they live.

Before the late 15th century, when non-Indians first journeyed to what is now North America, most Indian tribes were not ruled by a single person. Instead, there were village chiefs, clan headmen, peace chiefs, war chiefs, and a host of other types of leaders, each with his or her own specific duties. These influential people not only decided political matters but also helped shape their tribe's social, cultural, and religious life. Usually, Indian leaders held their positions because they had won the respect of their peers. Indeed, if a leader's followers at any time decided that he or she was out of step with the will of the people, they felt free to look to someone else for advice and direction.

Thus, the greatest achievers in traditional Indian communities were men and women of extraordinary talent. They were not only skilled at navigating the deadly waters of tribal politics and cultural customs but also able to, directly or indirectly, make a positive and significant difference in the daily life of their followers.

7

From the beginning of their interaction with Native Americans, non-Indians failed to understand these features of Indian leadership. Early European explorers and settlers merely assumed that Indians had the same relationship with their leaders as non-Indians had with their kings and queens. European monarchs generally inherited their positions and ruled large nations however they chose, often with little regard for the desires or needs of their subjects. As a result, the settlers of Jamestown saw Pocahontas as a "princess" and Pilgrims dubbed Wampanoag leader Metacom "King Philip," envisioning them in roles very different from those in which their own people placed them.

As more and more non-Indians flocked to North America, the nature of Indian leadership gradually began to change. Influential Indians no longer had to take on the often considerable burden of pleasing only their own people; they also had to develop a strategy of dealing with the non-Indian newcomers. In a rapidly changing world, new types of Indian role models with new ideas and talents continually emerged. Some were warriors; others were peacemakers. Some held political positions within their tribes; others were writers, artists, religious prophets, or athletes. Although the demands of Indian leadership altered from generation to generation, several factors that determined which Indian people became prominent in the centuries after first contact remained the same.

Certain personal characteristics distinguished these Indians of achievement. They were intelligent, imaginative, practical, daring, shrewd, uncompromising, ruthless, and logical. They were constant in friendships, unrelenting in hatreds, affectionate with their relatives, and respectful to their God or gods. Of course, no single Native American leader embodied all these qualities, nor these qualities only. But it was these characteristics that allowed them to succeed.

The special skills and talents that certain Indians possessed also brought them to positions of importance. The life of Hiawatha, the legendary founder of the powerful Iroquois Confederacy, displays the value that oratorical ability had for many Indians in power.

The biography of Cochise, the 19th-century Apache chief, illustrates that leadership often required keen diplomatic skills not only in transactions among tribespeople but also in hardheaded negotiations with non-Indians. For others, such as Mohawk Joseph Brant and Navajo Peter MacDonald, a non-Indian education proved advantageous in their dealings with other peoples.

Sudden changes in circumstance were another crucial factor in determining who became influential in Indian communities. King Philip in the 1670s and Geronimo in the 1880s both came to power when their people were searching for someone to lead them into battle against white frontiersmen who had forced upon them a long series of indignities. Seeing the rising discontent of Indians of many tribes in the 1810s, Tecumseh and his brother, the Shawnee prophet Tenskwatawa, proclaimed a message of cultural revitalization that appealed to thousands. Other Indian achievers recognized cooperation with non-Indians as the most advantageous path during their lifetime. Sarah Winnemucca in the late 19th century bridged the gap of understanding between her people and their non-Indian neighbors through the publication of her autobiography *Life Among the Piutes*. Olympian Jim Thorpe in the early 20th century championed the assimilationist policies of the U.S. government and, with his own successes, demonstrated the accomplishments Indians could make in the non-Indian world. And Wilma Mankiller, principal chief of the Cherokees, continues to fight successfully for the rights of her people through the courts and through negotiation with federal officials.

Leadership among Native Americans, just as among all other peoples, can be understood only in the context of culture and history. But the centuries that Indians have had to cope with invasions of foreigners in their homelands have brought unique hardships and obstacles to the Native American individuals who most influenced and inspired others. Despite these challenges, there has never been a lack of Indian men and women equal to these tasks. With such strong leaders, it is no wonder that Native Americans remain such a vital part of this nation's cultural landscape.

*The U.S. delegation marches
into the Olympic stadium in
Stockholm, Sweden, at the start
of the fifth Olympiad in 1912.
The 1912 Olympics, involving
athletes from 28 nations, quickly
became a showcase for a 24-year-
old American, Jim Thorpe.*

1

THE GREATEST ATHLETE
IN THE WORLD

On July 6, 1912, before an overflow crowd of 30,000 spectators, an ensemble of athletes representing 28 nations marched proudly into a newly constructed stadium in Stockholm, Sweden. A 4,400-voice chorus filled the 2-tiered structure with music, and the parade of young competitors filed past the royal box, where King Gustav V of Sweden and other dignitaries were seated. It was quite a spectacle, a ceremony filled with excitement and anticipation.

Various speeches and presentations were made, each followed by a resounding cheer from the crowd. Then the king stood before all present—athletes, spectators, dignitaries, and newspaper reporters—to declare the games of the fifth Olympiad open. The stadium was immediately enveloped by a huge roar, which thrilled and exhilarated the assembled competitors. This was their moment; none had ever experienced anything quite like the Olympics.

The next afternoon, a swift and strong young American began to carve his niche into Olympic history. Jim Thorpe, a 24-year-old Sac and Fox Indian from Oklahoma Territory, came to the games with a national reputation as a standout athlete. His exploits as a football player at

Carlisle Indian School in Carlisle, Pennsylvania, were legendary. He was known as a multitalented star—a brilliant runner, kicker, passer, and defensive player. In track-and-field competition, he demonstrated the same kind of stunning versatility, dominating virtually every event that he entered. Now, at the fifth Olympiad, Thorpe was slated to participate in two daunting all-around contests, the pentathlon and the even more grueling decathlon.

In 1912, the pentathlon consisted of 5 track-and-field events: the running broad jump, javelin throw, 200-meter dash, discus throw, and 1,500-meter race. This multi-faceted event had been added to the 1912 Olympic schedule at the urging of the Swedes; all-around contests were supposed to be a forte of Scandinavian athletes. The Americans, on the other hand, had the reputation of being excellent specialists but poor multievent competitors.

The pentathlon began with the running broad jump, or long jump. Thorpe leaped to a first-place mark of 23 feet, 2 7/10 inches. The second event, the javelin throw, proved more troublesome for the young American, who placed fourth. But his performance was more than respectable—it was impressive. Thorpe had thrown a javelin for the first time only two months before, and this event was a specialty of the Scandinavians.

The 200-meter dash may have been the most thrilling race of the Olympics. Thorpe finished first with a time of 22.9 seconds, just 1/10 of a second ahead of 2 other American competitors, who tied for second. He then dominated the discus throw with a toss of 116 feet, 8 4/10 inches, nearly 3 feet farther than that of the nearest competitor.

The final event was the 1,500-meter run, a nearly mile-long test of stamina. The pace was fast, but Thorpe got off to a slow start. He kept behind in the pack and waited to make his move until midway into the second lap. By the start of the third lap, Thorpe was even with the leader; by the start of the fourth and final lap, he was all alone in front. He finished yards ahead of the runner-up, with a time of 4 minutes, 44.8 seconds.

Thorpe's four first-place and one fourth-place finishes earned him a score of seven points and the pentathlon gold medal. His result was 3 times better than the score of 21 recorded by the second-place pentathlete, Ferdinand Bie of Norway. James E. Sullivan, the American commissioner of the games and chairman of the Amateur Athletic Union (AAU), was delighted with Thorpe's domination of the event. As quoted in *The Best of the Athletic Boys: The White Man's Impact on Jim Thorpe*, Sullivan crowed:

Thorpe competes in the shot put during the 1912 Olympic decathlon. Thorpe won the event with a toss of more than 42 feet and went on to triumph in the decathlon, which is regarded by many as the ultimate test of athletic ability.

> [Thorpe's victory] answers the charge that Americans specialize in athletics. . . . It also answers the allegation that most of our runners are of foreign parentage for Thorpe is a real American if there ever was one.

The next day, while the other pentathletes recuperated, Thorpe took fourth place in the high jump. He also

competed in the long jump, finishing seventh. These, however, were merely tune-up contests to help keep him sharp while he looked ahead to the event he valued most—the decathlon. It began on July 13, six days after his pentathlon triumph.

Like the pentathlon, which was discontinued after the 1924 Paris Olympics, the decathlon was included in the 1912 Games as a way of displaying the Scandinavians' all-around prowess. Decathletes participate in 10 events: the 100-meter dash, long jump, shot put, high jump, 400-meter run, 110-meter hurdles, discus throw, pole vault, javelin throw, and 1,500-meter run. Competitors are awarded points for their performance in each element, according to a set of tables approved by the International Amateur Athletic Federation. Although the Olympic decathlon is still held today, it takes place over a period of two days rather than three.

The first three elements of the decathlon competition were contested in 1912 amid a torrent of rain. Thorpe placed third in the opening event, the 100-meter dash, and second in the running broad jump. As he entered the shot put competition, he sat in second place overall. Thorpe wanted to finish the first day on top, but to do so his efforts in this last event would have to be outstanding.

With first place hanging in the balance, Thorpe summoned all his strength and propelled the iron ball 42 feet, 5 9/20 inches, more than 2 1/2 feet longer than his closest rival had managed. The throw was more than long enough to move him into first place at the end of the decathlon's initial day, 245.20 points in front of the second-place competitor.

The next day, the weather was nearly perfect. After Thorpe placed first in the high jump and fourth in the 400-meter run, he astounded onlookers with his perfor-

Thorpe (second from left) gets off the mark in the 1,500-meter run, an event he dominated in both the pentathlon and the decathlon. At the far right is Avery Brundage, who later served as head of the International Olympic Committee (IOC) and supported the IOC's controversial decision to deprive Thorpe of his Olympic medals.

mance in the 110-meter hurdles. Thorpe's time of 15.6 seconds led the field by a full 0.6 seconds and outshone all Olympic decathletes for decades. At the 1948 Olympics, the decathlon gold medalist, Bob Mathias, placed first in the hurdles with a time of 15.7 seconds—an excellent finish but still 0.10 seconds slower than Thorpe's 1912 mark.

As the second day of the decathlon competition came to a close, Thorpe's lead had more than doubled, climbing to 550.67 points. The final day of the decathlon also was the final day of the Games, the day on which medals would be awarded to the victorious athletes. Four decathlon trials remained.

Thorpe finished second in the discus throw, third in the pole vault, and third in the javelin throw. With one event left—the 1,500-meter run—he had the gold medal virtually wrapped up. He had dominated this element in the pentathlon, but many spectators wondered whether these three days of grueling competition had taken their toll on Thorpe.

In less than five minutes, all doubts about Thorpe's stamina were erased. He ran the so-called metric mile in 4 minutes, 40.1 seconds—4.7 seconds better than his pentathlon time. After three long days, it was over. Thorpe had won the Olympic decathlon gold medal with a sky-high point total—8,412.95.

There is no doubt that Thorpe was competing against the best of athletes in 1912. In previous Olympics, the United States team had been drawn from small, elite athletic clubs. The fifth Olympiad marked the first time that the American participants were chosen at open tryouts held at three regional sites—Harvard University in Cambridge, Massachusetts, Chicago's Marshall Field, and Stanford University in California. As a consequence, this Olympic contingent was the best conditioned and most competitive group of athletes ever to represent the United States in an international meet.

Not only did Thorpe outshine his American competitors, he finished nearly 700 points ahead of the second-place finisher, Hugo Wieslander of Sweden. Furthermore, his performance was for 36 years unbeatable; his score would have earned him a silver medal in the 1948 Olympics.

According to Robert W. Wheeler's biography *Jim Thorpe: World's Greatest Athlete*, Thorpe was never apprehensive about the outcome of his performance in the fifth Olympiad. "At no time during the competition," Thorpe later remarked, "was I worried or nervous. I had trained well and hard and had confidence in my ability. I felt that I would win."

The story of Thorpe's life is entangled with legends and shrouded by myths. One of the most persistent and unfortunate of these unfounded anecdotes is the oft-repeated story that Thorpe refused to train aboard ship and instead spent the 10-day journey across the Atlantic Ocean drinking and sleeping.

Undoubtedly, this story stems from Thorpe's fame as a so-called natural athlete; he did not train, so the argument goes, because he did not have to train. Ralph Craig, who won gold medals in the 100-meter and 200-meter dashes in Stockholm, was incensed by what he called the "backhand compliment" that Thorpe did not train prior to the games. "I can certainly remember running laps and doing calisthenics with Jim every day on the ship," Craig insisted years later. "In fact, Jim and I nearly overdid it on more than one occasion because we were always challenging one another in the sprints."

It is always tempting for sportswriters and historians to overstate the level of such a person's natural ability. But although natural talent might carry a person through informal races on the playground or in gym class, no one can reach the Olympics, much less hope to win a gold medal, without having developed and honed these natural skills. That, of course, requires long, arduous hours of practice and training.

Perhaps there never was an athlete more gifted than Jim Thorpe. Like all successful "natural" athletes, however, Thorpe knew that it took hard work to refine these gifts. And his track and football coach at Carlisle Indian School, the renowned Glenn "Pop" Warner, who accompanied Thorpe on the ship, would surely not let the talented young competitor forget it. Of course, the proof of Thorpe's training was his performance during the Games themselves.

When the fifth Olympiad ended, Thorpe had captured gold medals in the two most grueling track-and-field events. The medal ceremonies commenced shortly after Thorpe's win in the 1,500-meter run closed out the

Thorpe running laps on the SS Finlandia, *en route to Stockholm. Thorpe's natural ability gave rise to the legend that he never needed to train, but this photo and the testimony of his teammates indicate that he pushed himself to reach his athletic peak.*

decathlon. Each medalist, in turn, stepped forward to receive honors from King Gustav V. The *New York Times* reported that "when James Thorpe, the Carlisle Indian and finest athlete in the world, appeared to claim the prizes for winning the pentathlon, there was a great burst of cheers, led by the King. The immense crowd cheered itself hoarse." The king placed a laurel wreath on Thorpe's head and presented him with his gold medal and a life-size bronze bust of the king.

Moments later, Thorpe again was called up, this time for the decathlon ceremony. Along with another laurel wreath and gold medal, the king presented him with a gift from the czar of Russia, a silver chalice in the shape of a Viking ship, 2 feet long, 8 inches high, and weighing 30 pounds. It was lined with gold and embedded with precious jewels.

Before Thorpe could walk away, the king grabbed his hand and uttered the sentence that was to follow Thorpe for the rest of his life. "Sir," he declared, "you are the greatest athlete in the world." Thorpe, never a man to stand on ceremony, answered simply and honestly, "Thanks, King."

From William H. Taft, the president of the United States, Thorpe received a letter of congratulations in which the chief executive proclaimed, "Your victory will serve as an incentive to all to improve those qualities which characterize the best type of American citizenship." Taft's praise, however, may have prompted a strange mixture of pride and bitterness within the young Sac and Fox Indian. Thorpe might have characterized American citizenship, as the president said, but in 1912, as a member of an Indian tribe, Jim Thorpe was not officially a citizen of the United States. Not until 1924, through an act of Congress, did Indian people enjoy the full rights of U.S. citizenship.

When Thorpe and the other members of the U.S. Olympic team returned to the United States, they were greeted with a hero's welcome. On August 16, Carlisle Indian School hailed Thorpe and his schoolmate Louis Tewanima, the silver medalist in the 10,000-meter run, with bands, speeches, games, and a crowd of more than 15,000, a huge turnout for the small Cumberland Valley community. One week later, Carlisle's favorite sons joined their other Olympic teammates in New York City for two days of festivities, including a theater party, a breakfast, a ticker tape parade down Fifth Avenue and Broadway to City Hall, and a private banquet. There were similar celebrations in Boston and Philadelphia.

King Gustav V of Sweden presenting Thorpe with his trophies at the conclusion of the 1912 Olympics. At the end of the ceremony, the king declared to Thorpe, "Sir, you are the greatest athlete in the world."

Thorpe was overwhelmed by the reception. "I heard people yelling my name," he reflected, "and I couldn't realize how one fellow could have so many friends." Whatever else he might have won or lost during his brilliant athletic career, and his often difficult later life, Jim Thorpe was never short of such friends. He would live on in their minds as the greatest athlete in the world.

2

BRIGHT PATH

At dawn on May 28, 1888, in a one-room cottonwood and hickory cabin south of Bellemont in Oklahoma Territory, twin boys were born. The mother and father, Charlotte and Hiram P. Thorpe, both mixed-blood Indians, named their sons James and Charles; the former was destined for fame, the latter for tragedy. James's Indian name was Wa-tho-huck, which in the Sac and Fox language means "Bright Path." Charles's Indian name is no longer remembered, the result of an aggressive campaign, conducted by the white authorities who ran the Indian school system, to erase Indian names and require the use of English ones.

Jim and Charlie, as they were commonly called, were inseparable companions, spending their days in the carefree pursuits of boyhood: fishing, trapping small animals, and playing games with their friends. "Our favorite game," Thorpe recalled, "was 'Follow the Leader.' Depending on the 'leader,' that can be made an exciting game. Many a time in following I had to swim rivers, climb trees and run under horses." Jim and his friends loved to swim. "I lived in water," he remembered fondly. "It is great exercise. For the development of muscle and wind I cannot recommend it too highly."

Jim Thorpe as a teenager. Growing up on a ranch in Oklahoma, young Jim learned to rope and ride at an early age. When not busy with chores or school, he loved to fish, swim, and play baseball.

23

Thorpe's boyhood was not all fun and games, however. His father was a rancher, and so, as the boy grew older and stronger, he was expected to help out with the chores, such as feeding the livestock. Soon, he learned to rope and break wild horses. "At ten I could handle the lasso," he noted with pride, "and at fifteen I had never met a wild one that I could not catch, saddle, and ride."

Between the games and the chores, daily life for young Jim was exhilarating and often exhausting. "I was in bed every night at nine," he observed, "not because I had to go, but because after the day's activities I was usually tired and wanted to go. And I slept until I was called and told to dress for school."

School was a fearsome place for many a young Indian child. Indian education during the 1890s was founded on rigid discipline, manual labor, and the attempt to absorb Indian children into mainstream American society by extinguishing their separate cultural identity. The agency boarding school to which Jim and Charlie were sent in the fall of 1894 was typical of this sort of unenlightened paternalism.

The use of English, rather than Indian languages, was mandatory. The students were issued drab, ill-fitting uniforms to wear. Boys who had been wearing their hair long, in the usual Indian manner, had to have it cut. The prayers and hymns of the white man's Christianity took the place of traditional forms of worship. In this light, it is, perhaps, not at all strange that Jim was a reluctant and rebellious student, an "incorrigible youngster," in the words of one of his teachers.

School quickly became unbearable for the restless boy. He longed to be free of the confining classroom, of the strange, uncomfortable dark uniform, and of the teachers' stern looks and harsh discipline. He wished he could once again roam the woods, fish the streams, and ride the plains. The companionship of his twin, Charlie, a far more willing pupil, and the guidance of his older brother, George, provided a steadying force. And then there was sports.

For young Jim and his friends, the most popular game was "prairie" baseball. "Teams would be chosen and the game would be played out in the field," he recalled. "That was the equivalent of what is called sand-lot baseball today. We were also interested in basketball, but we had no track." Apparently the school officials felt that running and jumping games were an Indian "pastime," not a white man's "sport." "Only the Indians participated in this type of activity and it was of an unofficial nature," he explained. Likewise, no "Indian ball," or lacrosse, as the French called it, was played at the school.

Jim quickly emerged as the best athlete in his age-group. Many of the adults believed that he had inherited his skill from his father. Every Saturday, informal "meets" were held on a green pasture near the Thorpe homestead. Families came from all over the area, bringing food for an evening feast. The afternoons were reserved for various athletic events in which the adult men competed, and Hiram Thorpe almost always emerged the victor. "My father," Jim recounted years later with a pride undiminished by the passage of time, "was the undisputed champion in sprinting, wrestling, swimming, high jumping, broad jumping, and horseback riding."

Jim's father was the son of Hiram G. Thorpe, an Irishman who had worked his way west as a trapper and trader and settled on the Sac and Fox Indian reservation in what is now the state of Kansas. There he married a young Indian woman named No-ten-o-quah, or Wind Woman. In 1850, she gave birth to Hiram P. Thorpe.

In 1869, the Sac and Fox were evicted from Kansas under the terms of a new treaty and relocated to Indian Territory, in the present-day state of Oklahoma. Hiram

Hiram G. Thorpe, Jim Thorpe's grandfather, was an Irishman who settled in the West during the mid-19th century and married a Sac and Fox woman, No-ten-o-quah. When the U.S. government removed the Sac and Fox from their land in 1869, Thorpe and his family resettled in present-day Oklahoma.

G. Thorpe, No-ten-o-quah, and their children were among those who left the village under the escort of federal troops. Just a generation earlier, the tribe had numbered more than 4,500; on this final trek, there were fewer than 400 Sac and Fox people. Only 10 percent of the new reserve, a 17-mile-wide strip between the North Canadian and Cimarron rivers, was suitable for growing crops. Summer after rainless summer, the Indians watched their crops wilt and die in the sunbaked, sandy soil of the southern Great Plains.

Having grown into adulthood, Hiram P. Thorpe, the son of Hiram G. and No-ten-o-quah, decided to live apart from the Sac and Fox agency trading center. He moved about 20 miles away to a place where the grass grew thicker and crops had a better chance of surviving. There Thorpe raised and traded horses.

No-ten-o-quah (Wind Woman), Jim Thorpe's grandmother, belonged to the Thunder Clan of the great Sac and Fox chief Black Hawk. Thorpe was always proud of his Indian ancestry; after becoming a celebrity, he often spoke out in favor of equal rights for American Indians.

In 1882, Hiram Thorpe married Charlotte Vieux, the 20-year-old daughter of a French father and an Indian mother of Potawatomi and Kickapoo blood. Generations earlier, French fur trappers and traders had greatly influenced the Potawatomis particularly in the area of religion. Charlotte Thorpe passed this devotion on to her children, steering each of them toward Catholicism.

Jim's father knew the value of physical strength and firmly believed in training the body; he passed this on to his sons. According to one of Jim's boyhood friends, Art Wakolee, "We never received any training [at the agency school]. That is why Jim's father trained him when he was a young boy. . . . He taught Jim how to exercise in order to build up every part of his body."

Hiram Thorpe also taught Jim about sportsmanship and fair play. Jim always played hard, but he never played

dirty, never tried to injure his opponents. "The athletes he played against," continued Wakolee, "loved him for his good sportsmanship."

In early May of 1896, not long before the twins' eighth birthday, Hiram Thorpe gave in to their never-ending pleas and agreed to take them along on a hunting trip. Despite their young age, he reasoned, his boys certainly knew how to handle a rifle; after all, he had taught them. Naturally, Jim and Charlie were elated.

On the morning that they were to leave, however, Charlie took sick with a fever. Jim had to accompany his father by himself. On the last day of the hunt, Jim took aim at a buck and brought it down with a single shot. According to Sac and Fox tradition, his father promised that once they returned home he would call the entire village to feast on his son's first kill.

However, when they arrived, they discovered that there would be no celebrating. Charlotte Thorpe met her husband and boy with the news that Charlie lay gravely ill in an infirmary 20 miles away. The three of them jumped into a wagon and raced to be with Charlie, but it was too late. Jim's twin brother had already died.

Charlie's death troubled Jim deeply. When it came time to return to school in the fall, the normally outgoing

An 1893 photograph of the government-run school on the Sac and Fox reservation in Oklahoma. Forced to attend this school at the age of six, Jim Thorpe rebelled against the iron discipline and drab uniforms; one of his teachers called him an "incorrigible youngster."

boy was withdrawn. His disenchantment with school increased, and he even stopped taking part in the prairie baseball games. Finally, near the end of fourth grade, Jim could no longer tolerate the confines and discipline of the classroom and ran away from school.

When he arrived home, Hiram Thorpe, a firm believer in formal education, hitched up the wagon, drove Jim back to the school, and left him at the front door. As soon as his father left, Jim walked in the front door, out the back door, and raced home again. By taking a shortcut, he was able to beat his surprised father back to the ranch.

Hiram Thorpe decided that there was only one way to keep his son in school. "I'm going to send you so far," he told Jim, "you will never find your way back home." In the fall of 1898, he enrolled his son in the Haskell Institute, an Indian school in the town of Lawrence, in the northeastern corner of Kansas, 300 miles away.

Haskell was founded on a military system. The boys and girls wore uniforms and were taught to march in military style. Students were taught academic subjects and were also expected to learn a trade. At first, Jim did his best to endure the loneliness and the rigid discipline. When he could no longer stand it, he resisted.

As at the agency school back home, sports became his refuge. Baseball was the big sport at Haskell, but it was here that Jim developed his love for football. For the younger boys, football was little more than just kicking and throwing a makeshift ball, perhaps a stocking stuffed with rags or grass and tied closed. They learned the basics of the game from one of the school disciplinarians.

Jim loved to watch the practice sessions of the varsity football team. One of the stars of the Haskell team, and Jim's hero, was a 200-pound fullback named Chauncey Archiquette. One day, Archiquette noticed the eager young boy running across the field and imitating the older players. After practice, he stopped to speak with

Jim, was impressed by how much the boy already knew about the game, and asked him if he would like his own football. Archiquette took him to the harness shop, sewed some leather straps together, and stuffed them with rags.

Now that he had a "real" football, Jim began to organize games among the other boys. He displayed both skill and leadership and soon was good enough to play alongside the older boys. Through football, Jim started to emerge from the shell of sadness into which he had retreated after Charlie died. Jim also improved his performance in the classroom; for the first time, he was regarded by his teachers as a good student.

Near the end of his second term at Haskell, however, Jim again left school. The reason, this time, was not restlessness but familial duty. He had heard that his father had been shot in a hunting accident and was dying. He ran into town and hopped a freight train. When the train came to a stop, Jim was discovered and told to jump off. He soon learned that he had stowed away on a northbound train and was headed in the wrong direction. He was now farther from home than before. The strong, resourceful young boy turned around and walked all the way home—a 270-mile trek that took him two weeks.

To his surprise and relief, he was greeted by his father. Hiram Thorpe had been injured, but in the time it took his son to reach home, he had recovered almost completely. He was glad to have Jim home, and Jim was relieved to find his father alive and well.

His serenity was short-lived, however. Just a few months later, tragedy again struck. Charlotte Thorpe, a woman who, as the saying goes, "was never sick a day in her life," came down with blood poisoning and died a week later. As he had done after the death of his twin brother less than 5 years earlier, Jim, now nearly 13 years old, turned his grief inward and became a loner.

Shortly after his mother's death, Jim and his father had a run-in over the boy's duties on the ranch. Hiram Thorpe had gone into town on business and returned in late afternoon to find his livestock scattered and unfed. Instead of tending to the herd, Jim had gone fishing with his older brother, George. When they finally arrived home, the boys received a sound thrashing from their father. "I deserved it," Jim admitted, "but I didn't feel like taking it."

Impetuously, the young Thorpe ran away to the Texas Panhandle, where he worked on a ranch, fixing fences and breaking wild horses. He wanted to prove, both to his father and to himself, that he was a man. He also wanted to save enough money to buy his own team of horses that he could bring back to Oklahoma. A few months later, Jim returned to Hiram Thorpe's farm with his fine team in tow. His father told him that he was

The entrance to the Haskell Institute, in Lawrence, Kansas. Tired of having Jim run away from the Sac and Fox school, Hiram Thorpe sent his son 300 miles away to Haskell: "I'm going to send you so far, you will never find your way back home," he vowed.

Jim Thorpe (right) as a student at Carlisle Indian School, which he began to attend at the age of 16. By this time, Jim had become accustomed to the discipline of school, and he relished the chance to play on Carlisle's top-flight football team.

sorry he had lost his temper and welcomed his prodigal son home.

Jim's help was needed around the farm. Instead of sending him back to Haskell, Hiram Thorpe, at the start of the 1901 term, enrolled his son in the one-room public school in Garden Grove, just three miles away. Jim was relieved to be able to remain with his father and family, even though his new school had neither football nor track, sports that he was beginning to master before he ran away from Haskell.

There was baseball, however. From spring to fall, almost every day after school and on Saturdays, the boys would get together, mark out a dusty diamond in an abandoned wheat field, and organize a pickup game. Jim was the hardest thrower, so he always pitched. Because there was a rim of timber beyond the outfield, a home run meant that the game would have to be stopped temporarily, as the players hunted for the missing ball. Jim, the best hitter, was responsible for most of these delays. He always joined the search, but not until he had rounded all the bases and crossed the plate.

Jim remained at the local school for three years. A week before completion of the 1903–4 term, he met a recruiter from Carlisle Indian School in Carlisle, Pennsylvania. Years earlier, the Carlisle football team, which was en route back east after a triumphant West Coast victory against the University of California, had stopped at Haskell for a visit. It had been quite a thrill for the football-struck youngster to rub elbows with this collection of champions and all-American stars, and he hoped that someday he might be one of them.

Carlisle also enjoyed a strong academic reputation among the Indian population. Indian girls and boys came there from all over the country to learn such trades as tailoring, carpentry, and stenography. To Thorpe and his people, however, Carlisle was more than just a federally supported vocational school. According to Verna Donegan Whistler, a teacher at the school, "All Indians looked to Carlisle as their university. It was their great ambition to send their children here."

Consequently, Hiram Thorpe was delighted when Jim told him that he wanted to go there. "Son," he said to Jim, "you are an Indian. I want you to show other races what an Indian can do." At Carlisle, he would have that chance. At the age of 16, Jim Thorpe headed for Pennsylvania's Cumberland Valley and the beginning of a successful sports career.

3

A CARLISLE INDIAN

Located on the northern edge of town, Carlisle Indian School was founded in 1879. It was the brainchild of Richard Henry Pratt, a most unusual army officer. Through his military experiences, Pratt developed a unique sympathy for the interests of minority people. After the Civil War, he served with the 10th Cavalry, the so-called Buffalo Soldiers, a black regiment commanded by white officers. Eight years later, Pratt was transferred to Fort Marion in St. Augustine, Florida, where he was put in charge of Cheyenne, Arapaho, Comanche, and Kiowa prisoners of war.

Pratt treated his Indian charges with kindness and genuine concern, and they came to regard him as more of a counselor and instructor than a jailer. According to the officer, a group of chiefs who were being held at the fort came to him with a request. "We want you to teach us the way of the white man," they supposedly told him, ". . . then we will go anywhere you say and learn to support ourselves as the white men do."

The facilities at the fort, Pratt realized, were woefully inadequate for this purpose, so he set out to build a suitable school. After three years at Fort Marion during which he lobbied federal officials for funds, Pratt was able to convince the secretary of the interior to set up a

35

school for Indian boys and girls in the abandoned army barracks in Carlisle.

The project was assured of success when Spotted Tail, the chief of the Brule Sioux, entrusted five of his children to Pratt. Then other members of Spotted Tail's tribe followed their chief's lead. In 1879, Carlisle Indian School opened with 147 students.

Pratt's theory of Indian education, although well meaning, was based on rather condescending and paternalistic notions. To him, "educating" the Indians meant training them in the white man's culture and way of life so that they might be absorbed smoothly into the mainstream of American society. "I believe in immersing the Indians in our civilization," he explained, "and when we get them under, holding them there until they are thoroughly soaked."

Consequently, Pratt's program for Indian education required Indian youngsters to give up the ways of their ancestors. In an article entitled "Why Not Let the Indian Boy Keep His Long Hair and the Girl Her Dress?" which appeared in a Carlisle student publication, he wrote, "There is a great amount of sentiment among Indian teachers, but in the work of breaking up Indian customs there is no room for sentiment." In Pratt's view, Indian students should be taught, and even forced, to abandon their traditional practices "for their own good."

Carlisle's students ranged in age from 10 to 25. Half the day they were taught the usual academic subjects, and the rest of the time they worked at learning their chosen trade. They were required to speak English at all times and could be punished if they were heard conversing in their own languages.

Pratt ran the school as if he were training an army. All the students wore uniforms, drilled, had inspections, and awakened and went to sleep at the sound of the bugle. This regimen, Pratt believed, would give his charges the sense of order and discipline that they needed to get along in the white man's world.

The 16-year-old Jim Thorpe arrived at Carlisle in June 1904. He had hoped to become an electrician, but Carlisle did not offer a course in that trade. The school administrators decided that Jim had a strong aptitude for tailoring, so this became his area of vocational study.

Not surprisingly, Jim was awed by Carlisle's football reputation and hoped to make the varsity team. However, at 5 feet 5 1/2 inches and 115 pounds, he still was too small to play with the bigger, older students on the varsity squad. Disappointed but not discouraged, Jim tried out

Richard Henry Pratt (1840–1924), shown here as an officer in the U.S. Army, founded Carlisle Indian School in 1879. Assigned to supervise Indian prisoners in Florida, Pratt discovered that the Indians possessed a "high sense of honor," and he decided that they would benefit from a traditional education.

Three Carlisle students—Watte, Keise-te-wa, and He-ri-te—in their traditional garb. Like other schools run by whites, Carlisle required that the students wear uniforms, cut their hair, and adopt European names.

for the tailor-shop team, one of the many intramural squads at the football-crazed school. He made the squad as a starting guard.

But just as it appeared that Jim was becoming settled in his new environment, tragedy again disrupted the young man's life. Shortly after beginning his studies, he learned that his father had died of septicemia, or blood poisoning, contracted during a hunting trip. To make matters worse, because transportation between Pennsylvania and Oklahoma was dreadfully slow, he would not be able to return home in time for the funeral.

Although he was immersed in the rigid regimen of Carlisle campus life, Jim became more withdrawn than ever and did not mix with his new companions. It was

The same students—now known as Sheldon Jackson, John Shields, and Harvey Townsend—in the Carlisle school uniform. In addition to changing the students' names and dress, Carlisle sent them to live with white families during the summer to help them learn English and the "customs of civilized life."

evident to school authorities that Jim was consumed with grief, and they soon grew concerned for his well-being.

A unique feature of Carlisle was its so-called outing system, Pratt's most famous innovation. In this program, Indian boys and girls were placed in the homes of white families, where they performed chores. Usually, an outing lasted for the three summer months, but under special circumstances it could be extended for as long as two years. The practice reflected both Pratt's paternalism and his idealism; according to the school's Outing Code, which Pratt formulated, "pupils are placed in families to learn English and the customs of civilized life."

In his standard talk to the candidates for an outing, Pratt would tell them, "When you boys and girls go out on jobs, you don't go as employees—you go and become part of the family." Indeed, the families were expected to treat the Carlisle students as members of their household. Still, much of the time, the students were made to feel more like servants or hired help, and cut-rate ones at that. The students were paid wages, which were very low, barely half of what a white domestic servant or farmhand could earn doing the same work. And the bulk of a student's earnings were held in trust by the school.

Although Jim had been at his studies for only two months, the school authorities decided that in light of the recent death of his father, it would be best for Jim to take a temporary leave from Carlisle and live with a Quaker family nearby. He was sent on an extended outing to a farm in the town of Summerdale on the Susquehanna River, not far from Carlisle.

Jim wanted to work outdoors. After all, he had plenty of experience with physical labor, both on his father's ranch and on the Texas range; outdoor work had helped build him into a strong and rugged young man. Instead, his patron put him to work cleaning the house and helping in the kitchen, where he also had to eat his meals. The situation—and the meager five dollar monthly wage—left Jim humiliated and more unsettled than ever.

Eventually, the family with which Jim was living came to realize that this was not the kind of work for an active 16-year-old boy and requested a transfer for him. The following March, Jim finally was sent to a new farm, where he did gardening work. In September 1905, he was recommended for a more demanding and responsible position: foreman for the Indian workers on a farm in Robinsville, near Trenton, New Jersey. His monthly salary rose to eight dollars.

In the spring of 1907, Thorpe, almost 19, finally decided that he had had enough of planting endless rows of vegetables; he ran away from his outing assignment. When he was found by the school authorities, he was punished with a brief confinement in the Carlisle guardhouse.

By this time, Thorpe had grown to almost 5 feet 10 inches and weighed 144 pounds. More important, he was less withdrawn and sullen than he had been after his father's death; he began to display a newfound gregariousness and leadership ability. Furthermore, when he was readmitted to classes, he showed real improvement as a student. The poet Marianne Moore was a teacher at Carlisle and remembered Thorpe as "a little laborious,

Glenn "Pop" Warner, one of the all-time great football coaches, recruited Thorpe for the Carlisle track team in 1907. Warner at first refused to let Thorpe play football, fearing that he would be injured; when he saw Thorpe carry the ball in practice, he quickly changed his mind.

The 1909 Carlisle track team. Thorpe (back row, center) excelled as a sprinter, hurdler, and high jumper—a combination of skills that would lead to his Olympic victories three years later.

but dependable; [he] took time . . . [and] wrote a fine, even clerical hand—every character legible."

That same April, shortly after his release from the guardhouse, Jim revealed his athletic talents to the school's legendary coach, Pop Warner. Together they would make football history at Carlisle Indian School.

Ironically, football had once been prohibited for a brief period at Carlisle. Less than a decade before Thorpe arrived at the school, a player had badly broken his leg in a game. Pratt, believing the sport too violent, even dangerous, reacted by banning football. The following year, however, about 40 former players met him at his office and beseeched him to rescind the ban. Pratt said he would do so under two conditions.

"First," he insisted, "that you never slug. . . . You will play fair straight through, and if the other fellows slug, you will in no case return it." The players assented, and

Pratt continued. "My other condition is this. That in the course of two, three, or four years you will develop your strength and ability to such a degree that you will whip the biggest football team in the country. What do you say to that?" Naturally, they all agreed.

In 1899, Pratt, having reinstated football at Carlisle, hired Glenn Scobey Warner as his coach. His mission was clear—make Carlisle into a clean, winning football power.

From 1891 to 1894, Warner, while a student at Cornell University, was known as one of the best guards in college football. He was the team captain and at age 25 the oldest player, so his teammates nicknamed him Pop. The name stuck with him the rest of his life. Before coming to Carlisle, Warner had built a solid, winning reputation, coaching at Iowa State College, the University of Georgia, and his alma mater.

Warner was a renowned gridiron innovator, the inventor of many plays and ploys. The most famous of these was the notorious "hidden ball trick," in which a player would receive a kickoff, hide the ball under his jersey while his teammates created a chaotic diversion, race toward the goal line, and, having crossed it, remove the ball and touch it down on the ground for a score.

Warner pulled the trick in 1903 against the dominant football power of the day, Harvard, and caught the Ivy Leaguers napping. It worked perfectly—Carlisle got an easy touchdown. Harvard, however, still won the game, 12–11.

Warner left Carlisle after the 1903 season and returned to Cornell, where he coached for three years. He came back to the Indian school in the spring of 1907, just in time to discover the youth who, in only a few years, would be hailed by kings and commoners alike as the world's greatest athlete.

The story of Warner's discovery of Jim Thorpe is the stuff of sports legend. One April evening, Thorpe and a group of students were walking to an informal intramural football game. On the way, he noticed the varsity track athletes practicing the high jump. The bar was set at 5 feet 9 inches, and none of them could clear it. He asked if he could try it. The trackmen snickered—until Thorpe cleared the bar on his first attempt.

Leaving the track team in a state of astonished disbelief, Thorpe and his friends went on to their game. The next day, he was summoned by Coach Warner, who along with his football duties supervised the track program. "Do you know what you have done?" the coach asked. "Nothing bad, I hope," replied Thorpe. "Bad," Warner growled, "Boy, you've just broken the school record!" Thorpe told the coach that he thought he could have done better if he had been wearing a track suit. Warner told him to go down to the clubhouse and get a track suit—he now was on the team.

Thorpe marked his track debut at the school's annual Arbor Day meet shortly thereafter by winning the 120-yard high hurdles and the high jump and finishing second in the 220-yard dash. Warner could see the extent of Thorpe's natural skills, but he also realized that the young athlete needed to develop and sharpen them. He assigned Albert Exendine, one of the school's established track and football stars, the task of grooming the raw but promising Thorpe. In time, Thorpe broke all of Exendine's track records, a tribute to his trainer's dedication as well as to his own ability.

For most Carlisle students, the coming of summer meant another outing assignment. However, Thorpe now was one of "Pop's boys," and he no longer had to worry about being sent off to the country to clean houses, cook meals, or plant vegetables. His new, privileged status as a varsity athlete meant that he could stay around the campus during the lazy summer months, engage in some light training, and play a little baseball, both at the school and in informally organized games in the vicinity.

On one occasion, Thorpe and a pickup team of Carlisle students played a game in Hershey, Pennsylvania. The players returned to the school with their "winnings"—an abundant supply of the town's world famous chocolates— and were very popular around the dormitories for the rest of the summer.

In September, Thorpe decided to try out for football. When Warner saw him suited up at the first practice, he was furious. "I'm only going to tell you once, Jim," the coach told the surprised 19 year old, "go back to the locker room and take that uniform off! You're my most valuable

Albert Exendine (left), shown here with Coach Warner, was a track and football star at Carlisle when Thorpe entered the school. Warner gave Exendine the task of passing on his athletic knowledge to the youngster, and by the end of his career at Carlisle, Thorpe had broken all of Exendine's track records.

Thorpe became a star for the Carlisle Indians in 1908. Pop Warner later wrote of his prized player: "He could go skidding through first and second defense, knock off a tackler, stop short and turn past another, ward off still another, and escape the entire pack; or, finally cornered, could go farther with a tackler than any man I ever knew."

trackman and I don't want you to get hurt playing football."

Thorpe, however, was determined to make the team. "All right, if that's the way you want it," snarled Warner. He decided to outsmart the stubborn youth. Warner assigned Thorpe, an excellent kicker, to kicking practice in order to keep his valued track star from any contact. But for two weeks, Thorpe pestered Warner to let him get into some real practice. Finally, the coach could stand it no more. "All right!" Warner bellowed. "Give the varsity some tackling practice."

This was the first time, Thorpe recalled, that his hands had touched a real football, not one made out of a stocking or leather straps hastily sewn together. He outran some of the would-be tacklers and upended the rest. Warner was amazed at first, then annoyed. "You're supposed to give the first team tackling practice, not run through them!" he shouted. "Nobody is going to tackle Jim!" Thorpe replied. To back up his boast, he did the same thing again. Warner knew what had to be done. He immediately added Thorpe to the varsity team.

The 1907 Carlisle football team, Warner later remarked, "was about as perfect a football machine as I ever sent on the field." The team amassed a record of 10 victories—including a 23–5 defeat of mighty Harvard—and just 1 loss. The Carlisle Indians outscored their opponents by the astounding total margin of 205 points.

As a new man on an established roster, Thorpe spent most of the early games on the bench, observing and learning the ins and outs of big-time collegiate-level football. He finally got to play in the Syracuse and Pennsylvania games, and when the starting right halfback was injured late in the season, he started against Princeton and Minnesota. In each contest, he played flawlessly, although unspectacularly. Stardom was still a year away for this new Carlisle Indian.

*Thorpe cruises to victory in
an intercollegiate track meet.
Dominating his opponents in a
wide variety of events, Thorpe
could have set a number of
records, but he had little interest
in statistics—winning was all
that mattered.*

4

STAR ATHLETE

Football helped Thorpe "find himself," as the popular saying goes. For him and many other Indian youths, the status of athlete was a sort of latter-day equivalent to the position of warrior that their grandfathers and great-grandfathers had held. To be recognized as an athlete meant respect, prestige, and fame among one's people.

In the classroom as well as on the playing field, sports seemed to bring out the best in Jim Thorpe. In April 1908, he received grades of Excellent in history, civics, grammar, literature, and form and numbers (geometry and fractions). In his industrial major, which he had changed from tailoring to painting, he received a rating of "good."

Thorpe also began to exhibit previously untapped leadership qualities. Once, his academic teacher had to be absent for a day and turned her class over to Thorpe. He took the responsibility seriously, and several of the students in his class felt that he might make a good teacher, a notion that would have shocked his instructors at the old agency school or the Haskell Institute.

Spring brought the opening of a new track season and record-setting performances by Thorpe. "If you can clear the high jump bar at 5 feet, 10 1/2 inches," Warner promised his high jumpers, "I'll take you to Philadelphia to compete in the Penn Relays," the country's most famous intercollegiate track-and-field meet.

Only Thorpe qualified, jumping 5 feet, 11 inches. At the actual meet, in Philadelphia, he tied for first with a jump of 6 feet, 1 inch. As was customary at the time, an official flipped a coin, and Thorpe was awarded the gold medal in the event.

The following week, in a dual meet against Syracuse, Thorpe placed first in five events—the high and low hurdles, high jump, broad jump, and shot put—and took second place in the hammer throw. In the Pennsylvania Intercollegiate Meet in Harrisburg and the Middle Atlantic Association Meet in Philadelphia, he dominated the field, winning every event that he entered—the high and low hurdles, high jump, broad jump, and hammer throw.

At a triangular meet against Dickinson and Swarthmore colleges he set a school record in the 220-yard hurdles with a time of 26 seconds. He eventually would get his personal best down to 23.8 seconds. Setting records, however, was not a priority with Thorpe, as his trainer, Albert Exendine, observed. "He didn't care about records as such," Exendine insisted. "He badly wanted to win. That was enough. In races sometimes he took the last hurdle far in front and then just trotted across the finish line."

After the end of the term, Thorpe took a brief summer vacation back in Oklahoma. However, he soon grew restless for Carlisle. Perhaps he realized that without the opportunities that the school afforded him, he, like many others at home, might be doomed to the poverty-stricken existence of a dirt farmer. Thorpe returned to Carlisle almost a month before the beginning of the fall term and began training for football. Having filled out to a solid 175 pounds, he was certain to start at left halfback as

Thorpe poses in suit and tie with Walter Battice, an official of the U.S. Bureau of Indian Affairs. The confidence Thorpe gained from sports carried over into his personal life: He excelled in the classroom and became a leader among his fellow students.

well as handle the bulk of the punting and placekicking duties.

During the 1908 football season, Thorpe began to show touches of true gridiron greatness. Carlisle easily romped through most of the early matchups in the schedule. A few of these were little more than warm-up games against prep schools and small colleges, but there also were a couple of real contenders, including Penn State and Syracuse. In each game, Thorpe's running, kicking, and passing contributed greatly to an eventual victory and a winning record.

In their sixth game of the season, the still undefeated Carlisle Indians faced the University of Pennsylvania Quakers on their home turf in Philadelphia. Penn, packed with all-Americans, was also undefeated to that point in the season; in their first 7 games they had scored a total of 104 points to their opponents' 4. And the Quakers were looking to avenge the 26–6 humiliation that Carlisle had handed them the previous season. Looking back, Thorpe called this contest "the toughest game in my twenty-two years of college and professional football."

Carlisle dominated Penn that day, coming out ahead in first downs (8 to 6), yardage gained (272 to 196), and fumbles lost (1 to 5). Thorpe scored the Indians' lone touchdown with a 40-yard run and kicked the point after to tie the game. (At that time, a touchdown was worth five points, plus one extra point, if successful; field goals were worth four points.) But the Quakers, having scored their only touchdown in the first half, were fortunate to come away with a stalemate—a Carlisle fumble on the

Thorpe hands off to a teammate during a Carlisle scrimmage in 1908, his first year as a starting halfback. The Indians battled their way to a 10–2–1 record in 1908, and Thorpe was named to Walter Camp's all-America team.

Penn 20-yard line late in the second half prevented a possible tie-breaking score. Once the final whistle blew and the dust cleared, the two weary teams staggered off the field with the score tied 6–6.

Two weeks later, Carlisle finally lost its first game of the season—a 17–0 shutout by Harvard. But even in defeat, Thorpe performed brilliantly, with a 65-yard run from scrimmage and a 55-yard pass play.

Carlisle completed its 1908 schedule with a grueling 15-day western road trip during which they played 4 games. After Minnesota edged them in the first game 11–6, the Indians handed decisive losses to the Universities of St. Louis and Nebraska. In the season closer, Thorpe's end runs were the only effective part of the Carlisle offense. Nevertheless, they were enough to lead the team to an 8–4 victory over the Rocky Mountain Conference champions, the University of Denver.

The Indians finished the season with a superb record of 10 wins, 2 losses, and 1 tie. They had outscored their opponents 212 to 55. For stellar efforts in his first season as a starting halfback, Thorpe was chosen by Walter Camp, the nation's leading football authority, as a third-team all-American.

During the winter, Thorpe played some basketball for the school team and competed in occasional indoor track meets. He continued to take full advantage of the privileges that went with being a star athlete and a big man on campus, to the annoyance of the school's new superintendent, Moses Friedman. In Friedman's opinion, Thorpe was "far from being a desirable student." Although that may have been an overstatement, it was true that Thorpe began to ignore the school's attendance requirements; he even disappeared from the campus for a few days in February and again in March. Of course, as one of Warner's "football boys," he was able to get away with this behavior.

During the 1909 track season, in a dual meet against Lafayette, Thorpe enjoyed his greatest day as a track athlete. He did not defeat the Lafayette team single-handedly, as the story now goes; the other five Carlisle trackmen competed brilliantly that day as well. Still, Thorpe's performance was in a class by itself. He won 6 gold medals—in the 120-yard hurdles, 220-yard low hurdles, broad jump, high jump, shot put, and discus—and in the 100-yard dash he won a bronze medal. As proof that his Lafayette triumph was no fluke, if any proof were needed, Thorpe went on to dominate every other meet that he entered that year.

One day, as summer approached, he met two Carlisle teammates who were on their way to North Carolina to play minor-league baseball with the Rocky Mount team. The lure of sports was irresistible, and Thorpe decided to tag along. When he got there, short of money, the team's manager offered him $15 a week to play third base.

Rocky Mount was the weakest team in the East Carolina League and was short of strong-armed hurlers, so before a game in Raleigh, the manager asked Thorpe if he wanted to pitch. Thorpe emerged as the team's best pitcher, winning 9 games and losing 10 for a winning percentage of .474, not great in itself but well above the team's dismal .315 mark. When not on the mound, Thorpe played mostly first base. He batted a respectable .253 in 44 games and was known for beating out infield grounders.

When the minor-league season ended in September, Thorpe did not return to Carlisle but instead went back to Oklahoma and his family. At Thanksgiving, he went to the University of St. Louis to watch Carlisle clobber the home team, 39–0. He spent the holiday with his old football pals and told them he would be back with them the next year; they all missed Thorpe, as their mediocre

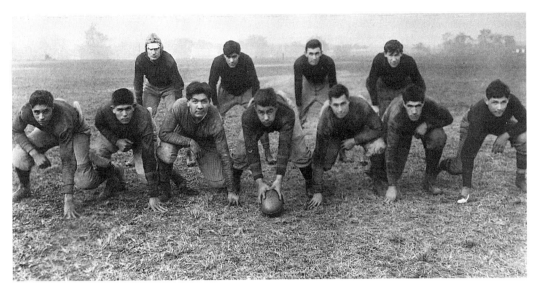

The 1912 Carlisle football squad, with Thorpe at the far right in the back row. After spending two years playing baseball and working on his father's farm, Thorpe returned to Carlisle and became a full-fledged star. In 1912, he was both team captain and a first-string all-American.

record that season testified. During Christmas he visited the Carlisle campus. This time, before he left for Oklahoma, he told his friends that he would return in time for track season that spring.

When the spring of 1910 arrived, however, Thorpe went back to North Carolina and signed on with the Fayetteville team. As a pitcher, he posted a 10–10 mark and batted .236 in 29 games. Thorpe's greatest asset as a baseball player, according to one of his Fayetteville teammates, Pete Boyle, was his incredible speed. "Thorpe did not burn up the league either as a pitcher or a first baseman," Boyle observed, "but he was a willing worker and was always valuable on account of his great speed. He could circle the bases like a deer."

The season was not half over when the club owner announced to the players that he would not be able to pay them for the previous week. They soon discovered that he would not be able to pay them ever again—the East Carolina League went under, and the teams were dissolved. Discouraged and broke, Thorpe slowly made his way back to Oklahoma.

Thorpe arrived in his hometown in early November. He made an attempt at farming but was feeling unsettled and restless. Soon he began drifting from town to town, almost 23 years old, with no purpose in life.

The following summer, in 1911, Albert Exendine was visiting relatives in Oklahoma. Walking down the street in Anadarko, a town about 50 miles southwest of Oklahoma City, he bumped into Thorpe. The erstwhile halfback was glad to see his old Carlisle schoolmate and track trainer.

Thorpe told Exendine that he had decided not to play minor-league ball that year. "Why don't you go back and finish Carlisle?" Exendine asked him. "They wouldn't want me there now," Thorpe replied. "You bet they would," his friend assured him. Exendine knew how badly Pop Warner needed Thorpe in his backfield.

Exendine phoned Warner, and before long the coach had sent someone to Oklahoma to escort Thorpe back to Carlisle and football. And, Exendine recalled, Warner had an ace up his sleeve. "Pop further induced Jim, although it wasn't necessary, by promising him an opportunity to qualify for the upcoming Olympic Games of 1912. We convinced him that there were no better facilities for training to be found than those at Carlisle."

Missing two full seasons of football did nothing to blunt Thorpe's skills. If anything, he was bigger, stronger, and faster than before. The 1911 season started like most others for Carlisle, with a series of warm-up games against weaker teams such as Lebanon Valley and Muhlenberg. In short order, the Carlisle Indians were 5–0.

The first big contest on the schedule was the University of Pittsburgh game in late October. The Carlisle team, by that point in the season, was honed to a sharp edge, and it used that edge to cut through the Pitt defense on the way to a 17–0 shutout. Thorpe really came into his own that day, carrying the ball on 2 out of every 3 plays and sending off punts of between 50 and 70 yards. Twice he was able to scramble downfield and recover his own punts; on one of these recoveries, he ran into the midst of 5 Pitt players, grabbed the ball, shook off would-be tacklers, and raced 20 yards for a Carlisle touchdown.

By this time, Thorpe's gridiron feats had begun to receive national attention. He scored a touchdown and kicked a field goal in Carlisle's 19–0 trouncing of Lafayette College. In the next game, a 16–0 victory over Penn, he also scored a touchdown. The sports pages of every paper in the country were hailing the exploits of Carlisle's star player. One sportswriter went so far as to call Thorpe "one of the best halfbacks in the history of the game." This statement proved to be prophetic.

On the second Saturday of November, the Carlisle Indians faced Warner's old nemesis, Harvard. In their 6 previous games, Harvard had given up a total of only 14 points. Carlisle was not worried, however; in their previous 8 games, they had given up just 10 points. The

Thorpe hurls the javelin during a 1912 intercollegiate track meet. Coming back from a three-year layoff, Thorpe used the college season to prepare for the 1912 Olympics, where his multiple skills earned him stunning triumphs in the pentathlon and the decathlon.

Carlisle Indians, never more ready for a game, scored points in all four quarters.

"This game," recalled Thorpe, "was one of the two greatest I ever played. The other was against West Point the next season." Thorpe carried the ball on 3 out of every 5 plays and placed 4 kicks through the goalposts, including one from 48 yards away. These field goals contributed 12 points. (By that time, the value of a field goal had been reduced to three points; touchdowns were still worth five points plus the extra point.) After the bitterly fought battle was over, Carlisle had prevailed, 18–15.

The next day, the *Boston American* put local partisanship aside and lauded Thorpe's performance as if he were one of the city's own sons. "He has placed his name in the Hall of Fame," the writer declared, "not only of Carlisle but also of the entire football world. It was indeed a pleasure to see a man not only live up to a great reputation but add to it through work beautifully accomplished."

As so often happens to young teams after a big game, the Carlisle Indians were listless the next week against powerful Syracuse. Their opponents primed themselves by chanting, "Get Thorpe! Get Thorpe! Get Thorpe!" Once the game began, however, they were unable to get Thorpe. He ran for two touchdowns but missed one of the extra points. Syracuse also scored 2 touchdowns but made both extra points and won 12–11. Thorpe, blaming himself for the defeat, was inconsolable.

Carlisle bounced back the next week against Johns Hopkins University. Thorpe played in the first two offensive series and scored each time. Then Warner pulled the entire first squad and played his second-stringers, who romped over the hapless team from Baltimore, 29–6.

In the season finale against Brown, Thorpe had a 40-yard run from scrimmage, kicked 2 field goals, and boomed an incredible punt of 83 yards. The Carlisle Indians finished the season with a near-perfect 11–1 record. On the train back to Pennsylvania, Thorpe's teammates elected him captain for the 1912 season. Walter Camp selected him as a first-team all-American halfback.

That winter, Thorpe wore his success and acclaim well and became more outgoing and jolly than anyone could remember. He played basketball, at least until it interfered with the indoor track season. And at Christmastime, he put on a Santa Claus suit and passed out toys to Indian children, who looked up to him as a hero.

Thorpe used the 1912 track season as a warm-up to that summer's Olympic Games in Stockholm, Sweden. He had not competed in track and field since 1909, but he performed as if he never had been away, overshadowing every competitor and winning multiple medals, usually gold. In June, he was given leave from Carlisle to train for the Olympics, which he did under Pop Warner's constant, watchful eye.

After his historic triumph at the Olympic Games, where he won gold medals in the pentathlon and the decathlon, Thorpe had one track "hurdle" left to clear—the 1912 AAU All-Around Championship, held in Celtic Park in Queens, New York. Like the Olympic decathlon, it was a 10-event competition; unlike the decathlon, which was stretched over 3 days, the all-around was held in a single day.

Thorpe was hampered by miserable weather and weakened by a bad case of ptomaine poisoning that he had contracted only a week earlier. Still, he not only won the championship, but his total of 7,476 points broke the old record of 7,385.

Joe Guyon, Thorpe, and Pete Calac (left to right) formed the backbone of Carlisle's powerful 1912 football squad. Perhaps the greatest of their triumphs that year was a 27–6 upset of Army.

The 1912 football season brought a number of major rule changes. The offense now would have 4 downs, rather than 3, to move the ball 10 yards and gain a first down. The field was shortened to 100 yards, and a 10-yard "pass zone" was added behind each goal. The previous 20-yard restriction on forward passes was abolished.

The new rules promoted more, and longer, passing plays. These changes suited perfectly the kind of wide-open offensive philosophy that, for years, Warner had employed at Carlisle. Because they were already familiar with this new, exciting style of football, the formidable Indians enjoyed an additional advantage over most of their opponents. As a result, 1912 would be Carlisle's—and Thorpe's—greatest season.

Thorpe and the other regulars did not see action until the third game of the schedule; the second team was good enough to crush Albright and Lebanon Valley by respective scores of 50–7 and 45–0. In his season debut against Dickinson, Thorpe ran for 2 touchdowns, including one that began deep in his own end zone and stretched 110 yards, the full length of the field. Carlisle won again, 34–0.

Three days later, against Villanova, Warner rested his starters and played his subs for the full game; they mauled their luckless opponents 65–0. The first team was back for the next game, against Washington and Jefferson College. This time Thorpe sparkled on defense, intercepting three passes. (In those days, football players had to play "both ways," that is, offense and defense.) His booming punts· kept the powerful Rose Bowl–bound Washington and Jefferson offense in poor field position and prevented them from scoring. However, Carlisle's offense was equally frustrated and could muster just a 0–0 tie.

After this brief setback, Carlisle and Thorpe regained their momentum and continued to roll over their opponents. He scored 3 touchdowns in a 33–0 shutout of Syracuse, and 3 more in a 45–8 defeat of Pitt the following week. In the first 7 games of the season, the Carlisle Indians shut out their opponents 5 times, scoring a total of 272 points and giving up only 15.

A 34–20 victory over Georgetown was followed by a very special event—the Carlisle team traveled to Canada to engage the University of Toronto rugby team in the first-ever international football game. Played mostly according to American rules, the game was, from the very first, never out of Carlisle's control. Thorpe ran 62 yards for a touchdown and punted for an average of 75 yards. The Indians won handily, 49–1. (Under Canadian rules, a team can score one point by means of a kick or a safety.)

Four days later, back in their home state, Carlisle visited Lehigh. Thorpe scored 28 of his team's 34 points, including a 110-yard touchdown run on an interception return. He also threw a near-touchdown pass. The ball sailed 67 yards in the air and was caught, but the receiver was tackled on the 1/2-yard line. The final score—Carlisle 34, Lehigh 14.

On November 9, 1912, Thorpe and Carlisle took the field in West Point, New York, to face the Cadets of the United States Military Academy. Like most of the Carlisle players, Pete Calac, the right tackle, was apprehensive about the game. "I didn't think we had much chance against Army that year," he noted. "They were very big, much bigger than we were. They thought we would be a pushover."

Pop Warner, who was as brilliant at psychology as he was at football, knew exactly what to say in order to inspire his players to perform up to, and perhaps beyond, their abilities. Years later, Gus Welch, the Indians' quarterback, still could remember his coach's pregame pep talk. "Warner had no trouble getting the boys keyed up for the game. He reminded the boys that it was the fathers and grandfathers of these Army players who fought the Indians. That was enough!"

Army came out keying on Thorpe, but he managed to get loose for big gains all day. Decades later, the story of Thorpe's performance has been clouded by myth and distorted beyond reality. But the facts are impressive enough. Although he did not score that day, Thorpe set up all four Carlisle touchdowns with his spectacular running. According to the *New York Times*, "He simply ran wild, while the Cadets tried in vain to stop his progress. It was like trying to clutch a shadow. . . . Thorpe went through the West Point line as if it were an open door." On defense, Thorpe's leadership kept the Cadets stymied for most of the game.

At one point, Thorpe received an Army punt on the Cadets' 45-yard line and ran it back through 11 would-be tacklers for what would have been a touchdown. Unfortunately, a Carlisle player was called for a penalty, and Army got to punt again. This time they wisely kicked away from the dangerous Thorpe. When the battle was over, Carlisle had defeated Army 27–6, and the Indians had enjoyed at least some symbolic revenge.

Starting at right halfback for Army that afternoon was Dwight David "Ike" Eisenhower, the future five-star general and U.S. president. Almost 55 years later, the

Future military hero and U.S. president Dwight D. Eisenhower started at halfback for Army in the Cadets' legendary encounter with Carlisle in November 1912. Recalling Thorpe's role in Carlisle's upset victory, Eisenhower later declared, "On the football field, there was no one like him in the world."

In addition to his brilliant running and passing, Thorpe was also famous for his booming punts and drop kicks. In 1912, he led the nation in scoring with a record-breaking 198 points and made first-string all-American for the second straight year.

former West Point cadet still recalled Thorpe's performance vividly. "On the football field," Ike insisted, "there was no one like him in the world. Against us he dominated all of the action."

Carlisle's next opponent, an unusually weak University of Pennsylvania squad with a 5–4 record, should have been no match for the 10–0–1 Indians. But Carlisle followed the upset of West Point with that dreaded, but not unexpected, letdown. The normally razor-sharp team lost its edge, and despite Thorpe's 2 touchdowns—1 running, 1 receiving—they were outplayed by Penn and lost 34– 26.

Carlisle rebounded a week later, due mostly to Thorpe, who scored all of the team's points—3 field goals, 4 touchdowns, 1 extra point—in a 30–24 victory over Springfield College. In the season closer against Brown University on Thanksgiving Day, Thorpe ran for 3 touchdowns and kicked 2 field goals, paving the way for Carlisle's 32–0 shutout.

The Carlisle Indians ended their magnificent 1912 season with a record of 12–1–1. They led the nation in scoring with a total of 504 points and allowed only 114. Thorpe himself accounted for 198 points, an all-time scoring record. For the second consecutive year, Walter Camp named Thorpe a first-team all-American.

Several years later, while coaching at Pittsburgh, Pop Warner enumerated Jim Thorpe's football talents.

> I never knew a football player who could penetrate a line as Thorpe could, nor did I ever know of a player who could see holes through which to break as did the big Indian. As for speed, none ever carried a pigskin down the field with the dazzling speed of Thorpe. . . . He knew everything a football player could be taught and then he could execute the play better than the coach ever dreamed of.

Of course, Warner's may not have been the most objective opinion on the subject of Jim Thorpe. Still, a more impartial source, the *New York Herald*, in an article published shortly after Thorpe's last game at Carlisle, echoed the coach's sentiments. "Jim Thorpe," the *Herald* declared, "appears to have possessed about every quality necessary to make a player close to perfection."

5

PROFESSIONAL STATUS

By mid-January 1913, Thorpe was back for what would have been his final term at Carlisle, basking in the glow of the previous year's glories, enjoying the attention that came with being an athletic hero. Over the next few weeks, however, he would become the object of a different kind of attention, one that brought not homage but humiliation.

During that dull period between the end of football season and the opening of baseball season, the time of year known to sports fans as the hot-stove league, a sports reporter from Pawtucket, Rhode Island, was looking for a story. During an otherwise uneventful interview with Charley Clancy, who happened to be Thorpe's manager at Fayetteville three summers earlier, the writer noticed a picture on the wall. "That's Jim Thorpe, the Olympic star!" he exclaimed. "What's he doing in the picture?" Without thinking, Clancy told the reporter that Thorpe had played baseball for him in 1910.

Clancy had inadvertently revealed to the reporter that Thorpe, prior to his successes at the 1912 Olympic Games, had been paid for playing baseball. Consequently, in violation of the Olympic rules, Thorpe was a "professional athlete." On January 22, the *Worcester Telegram*, a newspaper located in Worcester, Massachusetts, broke the story. In a matter of days, the news blared across the front

Jim Thorpe in the uniform of the New York Giants, whom he joined in 1912. Thorpe's Olympic fame enabled him to land a lucrative baseball contract, but his previous baseball earnings also led to the heartbreaking loss of his Olympic medals.

pages of every paper in America—Jim Thorpe was no amateur.

The question of amateurism is a tricky one. Contrary to popular belief, the athletes who participated in the original Olympic Games in ancient Greece were not amateurs. For a year prior to the competition, they were fully supported while they trained in their events.

The notion of "amateurism" actually originated in 19th-century England as a means of preventing working-class people from competing against aristocratic athletes. Because the wealthy did not have to worry about making a living, they could afford the luxury of being true amateurs. Everyone else in society had to make a choice—either give up precious training and competing time in order to earn a living or take money for athletic

The New York Herald *of January 28, 1913, announced that the AAU had branded Thorpe a professional because of his 1910 baseball salary and was depriving him of his Olympic trophies. The action was widely regarded as a grave injustice, but it was not reversed until 70 years had passed.*

performances and become a professional. If they chose the latter course, however, they would be ineligible for prestigious amateur competitions such as the Olympics. Not until the 1990s would the most elitist bulwarks of amateurism begin to be overturned, as the lords of the Olympics finally allowed so-called professionals into the Games.

When the story of Thorpe's professional stint in baseball hit the papers, the AAU immediately demanded a written statement from the gold medalist. He sent a letter—which was probably drafted by Pop Warner and Superintendent Friedman—to James E. Sullivan, the American commissioner of the 1912 Olympics and a top AAU official. In it, Thorpe admitted that the story was true and appealed for leniency:

> I did not play for the money, . . . but because I liked to play ball. I was not wise in the ways of the world and did not realize this was wrong, and that it would make me a professional in track sports.

It was a common practice at the time for college athletes to play professional sports during the summer, although they usually did so under assumed names. Had Thorpe been "wise in the ways of the world" he, too, might have played baseball under a pseudonym. Perhaps, as he insisted, he had been unaware of the rules of amateur athletics, or maybe he had had no intention of returning to Carlisle or of trying out for the Olympics. After all, it took a chance meeting with Exendine in 1911 to bring him back to school. If that were the case, there would have been little reason for Thorpe to conceal his identity.

In any event, Thorpe felt he had done nothing wrong. "I was doing what I knew several other college men had done," his letter to the AAU explained. He made very little money from his "crime"—no more than $25 or $30 a week. If he was guilty of anything, it was his love of sports. Thorpe pleaded with the amateur authorities to see it that way. "I have always liked sports and only played or run races for the fun of the things and never to earn money. . . . I hope the Amateur Athletic Union and the people will not be too hard in judging me."

The AAU's reply was sanctimonious and self-serving, absolving itself of any responsibility for the matter. The body's Olympic Selection Committee, it insisted, had chosen Thorpe "without the least suspicion . . . [of] any act of professionalism on Thorpe's part."

The organization was much harder on the unfortunate athlete. "Thorpe is deserving of the severest condemnation for concealing the fact that he had professionalized himself by receiving money for playing baseball," the authorities pronounced. The AAU apologized to the nations of the world for having allowed Thorpe to compete in the Olympics and promised to "do everything in its power to secure the return of prizes and readjustment of points won by him, and will immediately eliminate his records from the books."

The press and public reaction were totally behind Thorpe. The *Philadelphia Times*, for example, denounced the AAU for "'purifying' athletics by disgracing Thorpe and kicking up a muss that will be heralded the world over as a disgrace to this country." The *Buffalo Enquirer* criticized the hypocrisy of "AAU officials who think nothing of taking money for their services as managers of athletic meets" and defended college athletes such as Thorpe who attempted to support themselves during their summer breaks. The paper put it this way:

> Instead of hanging around all summer grafting pin money from their hard working parents, they went out and worked for their living playing baseball . . . , which is as fair a way as if they had been digging ditches or working on a farm pitching hay.

Thorpe (far right) poses with his New York Giants teammates. Despite his great strength, speed, and agility, Thorpe was competing against men who had years of experience in professional baseball. He had little success against major-league pitching and spent most of his first three years in the minors.

Even the international papers were sympathetic to Thorpe. The *Toronto Mail and Empire* cut right to the heart of the issue, arguing, "The distinction between amateurism and professionalism . . . [is] the modern counterpart of the distinction between Tweedledee and Tweedledum." And the Scandinavian papers unanimously told Thorpe that he should retain whatever he wanted.

Nevertheless, on Warner's advice, Thorpe did return his awards, which, according to friends, he later regretted. Contrary to the oft-repeated legend, Ferdinand Bie and Hugo Wieslander, the pentathlon and decathlon runners-up, respectively, did not refuse to accept the trophies. Still, they both maintained that if the decision ever were reversed, they would return the prizes to Thorpe.

Trying to put this sad incident behind him, Thorpe began to consider his future. Offers came in from fight promoters, vaudeville managers, theatrical agents, and motion picture producers. One showman offered him

$1,000 a week to perform feats of strength onstage. Show business, however, held little appeal for Thorpe; he was an athlete, not an entertainer.

On February 1, 1913, just 10 days after the Olympic "scandal" first broke, Thorpe sat in the office of John J. McGraw, the fiery manager of the New York Giants of baseball's National League. He had received offers from six major-league baseball clubs but eventually decided on the Giants. Although Thorpe's experience amounted to only 2 minor-league summers, McGraw promised him $6,000 a year for the next 3 years, a huge sum for an untried prospect. Later that day, Thorpe was dropped officially from the rolls at Carlisle.

The Giants were the best team in the National League, a baseball powerhouse whose lineup would be a tough one for any rookie to crack, no matter how many races he had won or touchdowns he had scored. Although

Thorpe and his bride, Iva Miller, photographed with ushers and bridesmaids at their wedding in October 1913. Thorpe's marriage was a source of comfort and support during the years that followed the loss of his Olympic medals.

Thorpe may not have realized it, the Giants signed him on as more of a drawing card than a starting outfielder. "If he can only hit in batting practice," McGraw confided to a friend, "the fans that will pay to see him will more than make up for his salary."

Playing in the company of a seasoned team such as the New York Giants, Thorpe's inexperience as a ballplayer quickly became evident. He could run well and throw hard, but his baseball skills lacked polish. Unaccustomed to the tricks of wily big-league pitchers, Thorpe's hitting was unremarkable. Soon after the start of the 1913 season, McGraw farmed him out to a minor-league team in Milwaukee, where Thorpe toiled for much of the next two seasons.

Thorpe would occasionally be recalled to the majors, but while there he spent most of his time on the bench. "I felt like a sitting hen, not a ballplayer," he complained. He saw little big-league action during the course of his contract with the Giants—19 games in 1913, 30 games in 1914, 17 games in 1915. His batting averages for those 3 years were a paltry .143, .194, and .231, respectively.

In October 1913, his first frustrating baseball season now behind him, Thorpe married Iva Miller, whom he had known and dated while at Carlisle. Although Miller had been a student at the Indian school, she was white. Her sister, Grace, was a teacher at the school and had become her guardian upon the death of their parents. In order to ensure Iva an education and acceptance to Carlisle, Grace had falsified enrollment papers. Only Iva's closest friends, like Thorpe, knew the truth.

For their honeymoon, Jim and Iva Thorpe toured Great Britain, Egypt, Italy, France, and Japan; Jim was then recalled to the Giants to participate in their traveling exhibition with the Chicago White Sox. Marriage with Iva would be a comfort to Jim in the troubled decade ahead. The couple had their first child, James, Jr., in 1915, and then three daughters—Gail, Charlotte, and Grace—during the next eight years of marriage.

Thorpe spent the entire 1916 season with Milwaukee, but he had a good year in the minors and was back with the Giants for their 1917 spring training camp. At the start of the season with the Giants, he was loaned out to the Cincinnati team. Away from McGraw, with whom he had never got along, Thorpe enjoyed newfound success at the plate—although his batting average was only .247, he amassed 8 triples, 4 home runs, 36 runs batted in, and 11 stolen bases in 77 games and 251 times at bat.

Near the end of the season, the Giants, in the midst of a pennant race, found themselves in need of bench strength and reacquired Thorpe. He came to bat 57 times but contributed little to the team's eventual first-place finish, hitting only .193.

Thorpe played with the Giants in 1918, but not long after the season began he experienced another personal tragedy. For three years, Thorpe's world had revolved around his young son. Suddenly, Jim, Jr., was stricken ill, either with infantile paralysis or influenza, and died. "After his death," said Al Schacht, a minor-league teammate who became a good friend, "Jim was never the same." Always a heavy drinker, Thorpe increasingly sought solace in alcohol and began missing practices. "He was heartbroken when that boy died," Iva Thorpe recalled. "His drinking problem increased after that."

For five years there had been a near-constant state of tension between McGraw, the stern disciplinarian, and the free-spirited Thorpe. The situation finally exploded early in 1919. While running the bases, Thorpe missed a signal, and his mistake cost the Giants a run. McGraw was furious and called him a "dumb Indian." Proud of his heritage, Thorpe would not tolerate racial insults and took off after McGraw. Some other players were able to restrain him, but his days with the Giants were over. He

Thorpe adored his young son, James, Jr., and was shattered when the boy died suddenly at the age of three. Friends believed that Thorpe never really recovered from this blow; after his son's death, he began to drink heavily, a problem that plagued him for the rest of his life.

was shipped to the Boston Braves, where his major-league career ended at the close of the season.

As a major-league baseball player, Thorpe was never the star performer that he had been on the gridiron or the track. It has been said, time and again, that he was "curve-balled" out of the majors. Schacht, however, disputed this, claiming that McGraw fabricated the story about Thorpe after their 1919 run-in. "When Jim was dismissed," Schacht maintained, "[McGraw] used the excuse of his inability to hit a curve ball, and the writers have echoed his statement ever since."

At first, Thorpe's lack of exposure to big-league caliber pitching did frustrate him. Still, in time, he began to master the art of hitting, as his record with Boston in

1919 shows. "I hit .327 [in 156 at bats] my last year in the National League," Thorpe noted. "I must have hit a few curve balls."

Over the next nine years, Thorpe logged a string of minor-league stops and generally hit the ball well. For example, he batted .360 with Akron in 1920, .358 with Toledo in 1921, and .306, with 3 home runs in one game, with Portland in 1922. He played his last official game in 1928 at the age of 40, with the Akron club.

In November 1915, Thorpe, resting up after another discouraging baseball season, was approached by sports promoter Jack Cusak, the manager of the Canton Bulldogs, a professional football team based in Canton, Ohio. Cusak offered to pay him $250 a game, an enormous sum for that time, if Thorpe would play for Canton in their 2 upcoming games against their archrivals, the Massillon Tigers. Naturally, Thorpe agreed—this sport was one he could handle.

Cusak's business advisers panicked. They feared that Cusak was leading the team into bankruptcy, but the promoter knew what he was doing:

> The deal paid off even beyond my greatest expectations. . . . Whereas our paid attendance averaged about 1,200 before we took him on, we filled the Massillon and Canton parks for the next two games—6,000 for the first and 8,000 for the second.

In baseball, Thorpe was more a gate attraction than a player. With Canton, he was both an attraction and a player. In the first game, Thorpe ran and caught the ball for long gains, but Massillon shut Canton out, 16–0. However, the Bulldogs won the following week's rematch, 6–0, on 2 successful kicks by Thorpe.

Thorpe's presence on the Bulldogs brought a new level of fan enthusiasm and profits to professional football, particularly in the town of Canton. Wisely, Cusak rein-

Thorpe (at left, about to assist in tackle) returned to football with the Canton Bulldogs in 1915. Thorpe's presence on the team drew thousands of extra fans to the games, more than compensating for his large salary.

vested his windfall gate receipts back into the team and added a new crop of college all-Americans to his squad. Thorpe joined the team after the second game of the 1916 season, once his baseball duties were finished, and served both as the starting halfback and the head coach. The revamped, powerful Bulldogs allowed just 7 points in their first 10 games and, led by Thorpe's running and kicking heroics, won them all.

In the next to last game on the schedule, at Massillon, the Tigers, who also were sporting a new lineup stocked with former college stars, held Canton to a scoreless tie in front of 10,000 fans. The following week, another 10,000 spectators watched the Bulldogs take their revenge, 24–0. In this pre–Super Bowl era, the Tigers were proclaimed—or, perhaps, proclaimed themselves—world champions of pro football.

In 1917, the Bulldogs again won the unofficial world championship. The First World War curtailed a great part of the 1918 season, but by the next autumn, the pro schedule was back to normal, and the Bulldogs were back in their usual position of dominance.

In the 1919 finale against Massillon, Thorpe kicked a 40-yard field goal late in the third quarter to break a scoreless deadlock. Moments later, after a failed Massillon placekick, Thorpe boomed a punt from the Canton five-yard line. The wind carried the ball through the air until it finally landed on the Tigers' goal line—95 yards away. Pinned deep in their own territory, Massillon was

Thorpe poses with Ralph Hay, the owner of the Bull-dogs. In 1920, a group of team owners met in Hay's Canton, Ohio, auto dealership to lay the foundations of the present-day National Football League. Thorpe was named president of the new league, though he had no official duties other than playing.

unable to score for the rest of the day. Thanks to Thorpe's powerful leg, the Bulldogs came away with a 3–0 win, an undefeated season, and another championship.

Although Thorpe continued to play baseball during these years, pro football increasingly became his main athletic interest. As in his Carlisle days, Thorpe was a superlative all-around player. He excelled on every aspect of offense—kicking, running, receiving, and even passing—and his defensive style was far ahead of his time.

Unlike most defenders of his day, Thorpe was no arm tackler. He hit like the defensive backs of today, by driving his shoulder, which was relatively unprotected, into the bodies and legs of opposing ball carriers. Often this punishing blow would cause a fumble, which Thorpe was always ready to pounce on.

The 1920 season marked the beginning of a new age in pro football. On September 17, owners of 12 professional teams met in the showroom of Ralph Hay's automobile dealership in Canton. (A year earlier, Hay had taken over the Canton Bulldogs when Cusak went into the oil business.) These men founded the American Professional Football Association (APFA), which, two years later, was renamed the National Football League.

The owners selected Thorpe, the biggest name in pro football, as the nominal president of the league. This position, however, was largely honorary and was meant to generate publicity for the fledgling enterprise, and he held it for just one year. The new league had its share of problems: insolvent franchises, no set schedules or official standings, a huge gap in quality between the best and the worst teams.

Thorpe's Canton Bulldogs finished with a mediocre 4–3–1 record, but at least the season was a personal success for him. His contract with the Bulldogs paid him $2,500 for the season plus a percentage of the gate receipts, well above the average player salary of $100 to $150 a game.

Prior to the start of the 1921 season, Toledo, Ohio, was granted membership in the APFA. The proposed team was to be run by Thorpe and baseball great Roger Bresnahan, but it never materialized. After these plans fell through, Thorpe joined the Cleveland Tigers as a player-coach and brought with him two Canton stars, former Carlisle Indians Peter Calac and Joe Guyon. Thorpe suffered broken ribs in a game in late October and missed almost all of the rest of the season. His team could muster only a dismal 3–5 finish.

For the 1922 season, Thorpe was a part of perhaps the most unusual team in pro football history—the Oorang Indians. Like many of the early pro teams, the club was created for commercial purposes. A dog breeder named Walter Lingo, the owner of the Oorang Airedale Kennels, wanted to promote his business.

Thorpe, who may have loved the hunting dogs even more than he loved football, was hired to organize and coach the squad. He lined up an entire team of full-blooded or mixed-blood Indian players, many of them former Carlisle teammates, like Calac and Guyon. The franchise was based in Marion, Ohio, but in its two years of existence it played all but one of its games on the road.

The Oorang Indians were a big gate attraction everywhere they traveled. Pregame and halftime shows featured Indian dances, hunting acts, and Airedale exhibitions. The players would take the field wearing war-bonnets and celebrate touchdowns with whoops and war dances, spectacles that by today's standards would be thought of as demeaning to Indians.

The caliber of the team's play, however, was not up to the level of its showmanship. The Indians struggled to records of 3–6 and 1–10 before disbanding after the 1923 season.

The Oorang Indians, shown here in a 1922 photo, were one of several sports ventures Thorpe undertook during the 1920s. The team consisted entirely of full-blooded or mixed-blood Indians, many of them former teammates of Thorpe's from Carlisle.

By 1924, when the 36-year-old Thorpe joined the Rock Island Independents, his football skills were fading. He still was a brilliant kicker, but as a halfback he showed only occasional glimpses of his once-great talent. More often than not, his attempts at running the ball were painful to watch. Thorpe started the 1925 season with the New York Giants football team. He was paid $200 per half, on the assumption—which proved to be largely correct—that he could not last for more than half a game. He finished the year back with Rock Island.

With his athletic career in obvious decline, Thorpe tried to bring some stability into his personal life. After the death of his son, Thorpe had grown increasingly estranged from his first wife, Iva, and the couple divorced in 1923. In October 1925, Thorpe married Freeda Kirkpatrick and regained a measure of domestic happiness. Jim and Freeda Thorpe had four sons: Carl Phillip, William, Richard, and John.

Thorpe was back with the Canton Bulldogs in 1926. His play may have lost most of its dazzle, but his name was still magic. Late in the schedule, the Bulldogs

traveled to New York to face the Brooklyn Lions. When it was announced that Thorpe would not play because he had broken two ribs earlier in the season, the hometown fans booed loudly. Late in the game, the Bulldogs—far behind—wanted to prevent a shutout. Thorpe entered the contest, to the delight of the spectators. The most he could accomplish was a 20-yard punt return, but that was enough to satisfy the crowd. They had seen Jim Thorpe and went home happy.

Thorpe and Freeda Kirkpatrick, shown here with two of their four sons, were married in 1925, two years after the breakup of Thorpe's first marriage. As his athletic skills eroded, Thorpe badly needed a stable home life while he sought other ways of making a living.

The 1926 campaign was essentially the last of Thorpe's football career. He did not play at all in 1927 and made a token appearance with the Chicago Cardinals on Thanksgiving Day the next year. Judging from the Associated Press (AP) account, however, he probably should have left the fans to their memories. "Jim Thorpe played a few minutes for the Cardinals," the wire service reported, "but was unable to get anywhere. In his forties and muscle-bound, Thorpe was a mere shadow of his former self."

Modern fans must keep in mind how Jim Thorpe and his early pro football comrades played the game. They were 60-minute players, old-time gladiators who went into their weekly battles stripped of most of the protective equipment and permissive substitution rules that benefit today's players. Under those conditions, to have withstood nearly two decades' worth of punishment on the college-level and professional playing fields was an accomplishment in itself. But to have done it with the kind of sustained brilliance that Thorpe achieved is evidence of a truly singular greatness.

6

HARD TIMES

Forty is a relatively young age in most lines of work. People in their early forties are generally considered to be in the middle of their career—on their way up. But in sports, athletes in their forties are on their way out, and adjusting to the end of an athletic career is usually quite difficult.

Thorpe had to face the challenge of starting over, of finding a new way to earn a living, at the age of 40. This task was made all the more difficult by the onset of the Great Depression in 1929, when the nation was hit with a tidal wave of unemployment.

In California, Thorpe sold the rights to his life story to Metro-Goldwyn-Mayer (MGM), one of the largest movie studios in Hollywood. He received only $1,500—a tiny amount for such a valuable property. The planned film, whose working title was *Red Son of Carlisle*, was never produced.

Thorpe took to trading on his celebrity. He refereed dance marathons—bizarre yet popular events in which couples competed for cash prizes by dancing around the clock. In early 1930, he was hired as master of ceremonies for an international cross-country marathon race. When the event went bankrupt, he had to sue the promoter for his $50 fee.

After his athletic career ended, Thorpe often had difficulty making a living. In 1931, a photographer found him working as a laborer in Los Angeles: "At least it will keep me fit," he told reporters.

A succession of menial, low-paying jobs followed. From February to October of that year, Thorpe worked as a painter for an oil company in Los Angeles. Luckily, he was able to remain anonymous in his labor. "No one knew me," he recalled, with apparent relief, "and I was lost in the oblivion of paint buckets and brushes while I painted filling stations and trucks."

When the job ended, he was able to secure some work in films, first in a bit part as Chief Black Crow in a picture for Universal Studios and then at MGM in a couple of sports movies. The movie work was sporadic, however, and soon he returned to physical labor, working on the excavation of the new Los Angeles County Hospital for 50 cents an hour.

The 1932 Olympics were held in Los Angeles, where Thorpe was living. Shortly before they were held, it was reported in the press that this once-great athlete could not afford the price of a ticket. People from all over the country responded to this sad story and offered to send money so that Thorpe could attend the Games.

The Olympics were to be proclaimed open by Vice-president Charles Curtis. A man of Indian heritage, Curtis insisted that Thorpe sit with him. As the world's greatest athlete took his seat in the Los Angeles Coliseum, the capacity crowd of 105,000 greeted him with a standing ovation.

After the Olympics, it was back to small roles and extra work in "B" movies, usually westerns. By the mid-1930s, the film industry began to climb out of the depression. Thorpe not only was able to work more often, but the quality of the movies improved, as did the roles he was hired to play.

In 1937, Thorpe returned to Oklahoma and traveled among the Sac and Fox, campaigning to abolish the Bureau of Indian Affairs. In his view, the agency did little

Thorpe (center) portrays Chief Red Smoke in the Warner Bros. western Treachery Rides the Range. *Thorpe appeared in a number of films during the 1930s; although MGM bought the rights to his life story, the projected film,* Red Son of Carlisle, *was never produced.*

except hold back his people's political and social progress. Thorpe called on Congress to pass the Wheeler Bill, which would have abolished the bureau and transferred the management of Indian issues to a new, all-Indian body. He wrote:

> The 6,000 [federal bureaucrats] now employed in political jobs administering Indian affairs should be dismissed and the Indians should begin management of their own business. . . . The Indian should be permitted to shed his inferiority complex and live like a normal American citizen.

The bill, however, was defeated in the House of Representatives.

Because of his athletic accomplishments, Thorpe became a popular public speaker. Through the end of the 1930s and into the 1940s, he combined film work with speaking engagements all around the country. In an average week, he would give four lectures; sometimes, he might give three in a single day. Typically, Thorpe, dressed in an Indian costume, would begin his talks with a few anecdotes about his football or track career. Then, having warmed up his audience, he would proceed to speak on a subject about which he cared very deeply—American Indians.

Thorpe with two of his dogs, Spot and Bugler, in 1940. Thorpe had a lifelong love of hunting dogs. His daughter Grace recalled that as many as 18 dogs occupied the family's backyard, much to the distress of the neighbors.

Thorpe's lecture career improved his financial situation somewhat. However, it kept him away from his home and family for extended periods of time. In 1941, his second wife, Freeda, sued for divorce on the grounds of negligence. Years later, however, Freeda Thorpe revealed that the traveling was not the primary reason that she decided to end the marriage. "It was mainly the drinking," she explained. "I could adjust to him being away . . . but the drinking was the main problem."

For many years, Thorpe had been a heavy drinker. Perhaps he inherited the problem from his father, Hiram, a pleasant man when sober, but a ferocious one when drunk—which he often was. Or perhaps it was Thorpe's way to escape, although only temporarily, the tragedies and disappointments that dotted his life—the loss of his Olympic medals, the death of his first son, the ignominious way in which he had had to earn a living once the glory days were over. In any event, alcohol became an increasingly frequent companion for Thorpe, and it often led him into trouble.

Thorpe always was careless with money, and his drinking made matters only worse. Alcohol tended to turn Thorpe's natural kindness and generosity into a naive gullibility. In bars, he was an easy mark for "loans" that were never repaid and investment schemes that never paid off.

When sober, however, Thorpe would display his lifelong capacity for enjoying the simple things. He loved to take his boys rabbit and raccoon hunting in California's Santa Ana Mountains. Thorpe drove his old cars until they fell apart, and they always seemed to be filled with children and dogs. He spent long days on chartered boats fishing the Pacific coast for mackerel. He was still a strong swimmer, and his impromptu kicking demonstrations on local school playgrounds and football fields are legendary.

He would talk and joke about practically everything, except the lost gold medals—according to friends, he never mentioned them.

In December 1941, the United States entered the Second World War, and Thorpe desperately wanted to serve his country. He was, however, 53 years old—too old for active military duty. Harry Bennett, right-hand man to auto manufacturer Henry Ford, learned of Thorpe's desire to take part in the war effort, and the following March, Bennett brought him to Ford's River Rouge plant in Dearborn, Michigan. There Thorpe worked plant security on a staff composed entirely of athletes—boxers, baseball players, and, at one point, the entire University of Michigan football team, including their head coach.

The following February, Thorpe suffered his first heart attack. When he left the hospital, he went back to Oklahoma for a recuperative vacation. He resigned his job at Ford in November 1943 and stayed in Oklahoma with friends.

In June 1945, Thorpe married Patricia Gladys Askew. World War II was virtually over, but, unexpectedly, Thorpe was accepted for duty in the merchant marine. He was assigned to the USS *Southwest Victory*, which departed for India carrying ammunition to the American and British troops. "We had some rough weather and some rough times," he remembered, "but we had team-work."

Aboard ship, Thorpe worked, anonymously at first, as the ship's carpenter. When they landed in Calcutta, a number of high-ranking military officials, including a few former athletes from West Point, came to visit him. "The Captain of the ship couldn't figure it out," he laughed. "He was not able to understand why brigadier generals and people like that would be glad to see

During the 1940s, Thorpe lectured widely, urging physical fitness programs for young people. In this 1948 photograph, he set the pace for a group of runners in a Junior Olympics held on Chicago's tough South Side.

someone who was as far down in the ship as I was." The brass asked Thorpe to appear before the troops, and he agreed. He spent the next few days touring military installations in the area.

Thorpe returned to the United States in September and resumed his personal appearances. Previously, his lecture fees had been small—when he received any payment at all. His new wife, Patricia, a shrewd businesswoman, remedied that matter. Under her guidance, Thorpe began to charge $500 plus expenses for each personal appearance. "But though there was more money around the house," Thorpe's son Carl observed, "it seemed to me that it was going to her for things like diamond rings and furs. As far as Dad was concerned, as long as he had a buck for the next day, he was fine."

His favorite topic during the postwar years was physical fitness, especially for young people. "We should have a boys' and girls' Olympics each year," he urged. He saw athletics as the solution to the problem of juvenile delinquency. "Sports," he reasoned, "will improve health and keep the children out of trouble." In March 1948, Thorpe began to put his idea into practice. He joined the recreation staff of the Chicago Park District and appeared throughout the city, teaching the fundamentals of track to eager young people.

At the age of 60, Thorpe shows the crowd at New York's Polo Grounds that he can still kick a football. Appearing during halftime of a soccer game, the former all-American booted 3 field goals from the 50-yard line.

That August, Thorpe traveled to San Francisco to be honored along with his old mentor Pop Warner and fellow football great Ernie Nevers. After the first half of that weekend's San Francisco 49ers–Baltimore Colts game, the 60-year-old Thorpe donned a uniform and put on a field goal kicking exhibition for the crowd.

Not long after his trip to San Francisco, Thorpe took on an unusual assignment. He was hired to prepare Israel's National Soccer Team for a late September match against the U.S. Olympic Soccer Team at the Polo Grounds in New York City. On the day of the game, he gave another halftime kicking exhibition. Standing at the 50-yard line, he drop-kicked 3 of 10 attempts over the crossbar and then punted twice in each direction, the first for 70 yards and the second for 75.

The 1930s and 1940s were an often difficult period for Thorpe. "I cannot decide," the man whose Sac and Fox name was Bright Path once reflected, "whether I was well named or not. Many a time the path has gleamed bright for me, but just as often it has been dark and bitter indeed." But by the end of the 1940s, at least some of the brightness was returning to Jim Thorpe's life.

7

FINAL GLORY

As the midpoint of the 20th century neared, Thorpe's celebrity underwent something of a revival. In January 1950, an AP poll of 391 sportswriters and broadcasters selected him as the Greatest Football Player of the Half-Century. A little more than two weeks later, similar AP poll went even further, naming Thorpe the Greatest Athlete of the Half-Century.

In the AP's voting system, he received a total of 875 points and was the first choice of 252 of the 391 respondents, far ahead of the second- and third-place selections, baseball legend Babe Ruth (539 points and 86 first-place votes) and heavyweight boxer Jack Dempsey (246 points, 19 firsts).

The previous August, Warner Brothers studios announced that it had purchased from MGM the long-dormant film rights to Thorpe's life story. Unfortunately, Thorpe made no money from the deal. The contract he had signed with MGM 20 years earlier gave him no rights in the event of such a resale.

The studio did hire him to serve as "technical adviser" to the picture. Burt Lancaster, who portrayed the athlete in the movie, recalled that Thorpe helped him with the basics of kicking a football. However, according to the actor, "Jim was kept around the set . . . , but the job was

Thorpe rides in a motorcade in Carlisle, Pennsylvania, in 1951. As the years went by and Thorpe's feats remained unmatched, the press and the public began to appreciate his true athletic greatness.

95

a manufactured one. They really didn't know what to do with him, which is generally the case when you do anyone's life who happens to be alive."

The film, *Jim Thorpe—All-American*, premiered in two cities, Oklahoma City and Carlisle, on August 23, 1951. That same month, Thorpe was inducted into the National College Football Hall of Fame in New York City. He attended the Carlisle premiere with his eldest son, Carl Phillip; Phyllis Thaxter, who played his first wife in the film; the governor of Pennsylvania; and assorted celebrities and dignitaries.

Carlisle Indian School had been closed since 1918—it became the Army War College—but the people of the town still remembered Thorpe's heroics. A monument was unveiled at the courthouse that read:

> In Recognition of the Athletic Achievements of JIM THORPE Student of the Carlisle Indian School, Olympic Champion at Stockholm in 1912 and in 1950 Voted the Greatest Football Player and Athlete of the First Half of the 20th Century.

Like most film biographies, *Jim Thorpe—All-American* presented a rather distorted account of its subject's actual life. Lancaster gave a fine performance, but the story line is strewn with Hollywood clichés: The mother wants her son to be a success in life, the young man takes up football to impress the girl he likes, and key racial issues are played down.

Eventually, the plot sinks into pathos and melodrama, as when Thorpe is shown forlornly watching the 1932 Olympics, having taken to drink at the death of his first son and unable to hold down a job. Still, the film concludes on the inevitable upbeat, with Pop Warner telling the fallen hero that the state of Oklahoma has decided to erect a monument to one of its favorite sons—"Jim Thorpe, the greatest athlete of them all."

Thorpe poses with golf champion Babe Didrikson Zaharias in 1950, after sportswriters voted them best male and female athletes of the half-century. In the poll, Thorpe finished well ahead of such legendary sports heroes as Babe Ruth and Jack Dempsey.

Despite all this, or perhaps because of it, *Jim Thorpe—All-American* was a box office hit.

In the midst of this renewed attention, a movement to restore Thorpe's Olympic medals was born. Since the late 1940s, leading sports figures, sportswriters, members of Congress, and even the International Association of Rotary Clubs had attempted to reason with the U.S. Olympic Committee and its president, Avery Brundage. Every attempt was frustrated.

In one of those rare occasions when he broke his silence on the matter, Thorpe complained to a reporter, "[Brundage] could get those things back for me, but so far, he just played shut-mouth." Brundage reckoned himself a man of principle, but the principles he defended most adamantly were the shaky rules of amateurism.

In 1952, Brundage became head of the International Olympic Committee, the throne from which he ruled the world of amateur sports for the next 20 years. To his death in 1975, he remained immovable on the question of reinstating Thorpe. Some sports historians have suggested that Brundage's refusal to help Thorpe may have stemmed from his own athletic disappointments. In 1912, he, not Thorpe, was America's pre-Olympic favorite in the pentathlon and decathlon. At Stockholm, however, Brundage could do no better than place sixth in the former event, and he failed to finish the latter at all.

In November 1951, three months after the release of the movie, Thorpe was in Philadelphia heading an all-Indian song and dance troupe. He noticed an infection on his lower lip. A few days later, it still had not healed, so he stopped by a local hospital to have it examined. It turned out to be cancer, but he had sought treatment in time and the tumor was removed with no aftereffects.

Thorpe, however, was broke again. To cover the hospital bills, Patricia Thorpe organized the Fair Play for Thorpe Committee and solicited contributions totaling more than $4,500. The campaign also brought a renewed, and again unsuccessful, call for the restoration of Thorpe's Olympic honors.

Thorpe remained in good health until the following September, 10 months after his surgery for lip cancer, when he had his second heart attack. He recovered quickly and was able to leave the hospital in less than three days. Then, on March 28, 1953, two months short of what would have been his 65th birthday, while eating lunch in the trailer where he lived in Lomita, California, Thorpe suffered a third and massive attack. A doctor was summoned, but there was nothing that could be done. Jim Thorpe was gone.

A Roman Catholic funeral service was held for Thorpe in California. Afterward, he was supposed to have been buried in his hometown, in Shawnee, Oklahoma. Ross Porter, the general manager and editor of the *Shawnee News Star*, headed up a campaign to raise $2,500 to bring the body there from California. State legislators sponsored a bill that would have appropriated $25,000 in state funding for the construction of a fitting monument to the great athlete. According to Porter, Governor William H. Murray had assured him that he would approve the measure. "Sure enough," Porter recalled, "it went through and within forty-eight hours it was on Murray's desk, and he double-crossed us and vetoed the bill."

Avery Brundage (second from left) confers with other members of the International Olympic Committee (IOC) in 1948. When Brundage became head of the IOC in 1952, he refused to advocate restoring Thorpe's medals. Some observers were convinced that Brundage still resented Thorpe's dominance of the 1912 Olympics.

The body was held in a temporary crypt, first in Shawnee, later in Tulsa. Then Patricia Thorpe heard about Mauch Chunk, Pennsylvania, a small town 90 miles north of Philadelphia. The residents had pledged a nickel a week to create a fund to bring new industry into their community. She traveled there, met Joe Boyle, editor of the local paper and leader of this industrial development campaign, and presented him with a scheme.

Although her late husband certainly never visited Mauch Chunk and probably never even heard of it, Patricia Thorpe proposed that if the town would change

Thorpe's third wife, Patricia, attends the unveiling of a monument to her late husband in Jim Thorpe, Pennsylvania, in 1957. The town had changed its name from Mauch Chunk and set up the memorial to Thorpe in the hope of attracting tourists, but the scheme never panned out.

its name to Jim Thorpe, she would move his body there and arrange to have a memorial constructed. Boyle felt that the plan might attract both industry and tourists to the economically sagging town, but he feared that the citizens might resist the name change. On the other hand, there were many people who wanted to consolidate Mauch Chunk with the neighboring town of East Mauch Chunk. He convinced other civic and business leaders that this plan could be the way to bring the two communities together. In a special election, the residents of the towns voted to become Jim Thorpe, Pennsylvania.

A red-granite mausoleum was constructed with money borrowed from the industrial development fund and was then dedicated on Memorial Day, 1957. The memorial is set on a grassy knoll along North Street (Route 903). On its front are inscribed the words of King Gustav V—"Sir, you are the greatest athlete in the world"—and on each side are etchings depicting Thorpe's Indian heritage and his various athletic pursuits.

From the first, Thorpe's children opposed Patricia Thorpe's plan. In the view of son Jack, "Dad's body was sold for a tourist attraction"—and an unsuccessful one at that, for the name change brought little industry or tourism into the town. Moreover, his children have insisted that according to Indian tradition, Thorpe's body must be returned to his native soil and given a proper Indian burial. Until it is, they believe, his soul is doomed to wander.

At the same time, some people in the town have voiced second thoughts about the decision, noting that the new name has brought them few economic benefits. "All we got here," one disgruntled citizen told a *Sports Illustrated* reporter, "is a dead Indian." In a 1964 election, a proposal to change the name back to Mauch Chunk lost, but only narrowly, by a vote of 1,392 to 1,032. The following year the same question lost by a similar margin. Despite the feelings of both Thorpe's descendants and some of the residents, officials maintain that the town will remain Jim Thorpe, Pennsylvania, and that Jim Thorpe will remain there.

In the years since his death, numerous honors have been bestowed upon Thorpe. In 1955, the National Football League named its annual most valuable player award the Jim Thorpe Trophy. Each year in college football, the season's best defensive back is presented with the Jim Thorpe Award. In 1958, Thorpe was elected to the National Indian Hall of Fame in Anadarko, Oklahoma, and in 1961 to the Pennsylvania Hall of Fame. The home in which he and his first wife, Iva, lived in Yale, Oklahoma, was purchased by the state and opened to the public. And Thorpe's portrait was hung in the rotunda of the state capitol.

In September 1963, Thorpe was inducted as a charter member of the Pro Football Hall of Fame in Canton, Ohio. (His old Carlisle and pro teammate, Joe Guyon, joined him there three years later.) Today the first sight that visitors encounter as they enter the Hall is a life-size statue of pro football's first big star, Jim Thorpe.

After decades of argument, the Amateur Athletic Union, in October 1973, finally reversed its 70-year-old position and restored Thorpe's amateur status for the period 1909–12. The way was then paved for the restoration of the gold medals, because it was a decision of the AAU, not the International Olympic Committee, that had stripped Thorpe of his awards.

In 1982, Thorpe biographer Robert Wheeler and his wife, Florence Ridlon, organized the Jim Thorpe Foundation, which was dedicated to two tasks—securing the return of his Olympic medals and educating the public about the accomplishments of this superlative athlete. As

Thorpe's statue dominates the lobby of the Pro Football Hall of Fame in Canton, Ohio. In recognition of Thorpe's achievements, each season's most valuable player in the National Football League is honored with the Jim Thorpe Trophy.

she was researching the bylaws of the 1912 Olympiad, Ridlon discovered Rule 13, which would become the basis of a successful appeal to reinstate Thorpe:

> Objections to the qualifications of a competitor must be made in writing . . . to the Swedish Olympic Committee. No such objection shall be entertained unless . . . received by the Swedish Olympic Committee before the lapse of 30 days from the distribution of prizes.

The newspaper story that caused Thorpe's disqualification did not appear until nearly seven months after the close of the Games. The rule-bound guardians of amateurism had violated their own regulations. For decades, Thorpe's supporters appealed to men such as James Sullivan and Avery Brundage, claiming that Thorpe was unaware of the rules governing amateur sports. Their answer was always the same: Ignorance is no excuse. Now Wheeler and Ridlon had an answer for the Sullivans and the Brundages—their own ignorance of Olympic rules was no excuse for depriving Thorpe of his rightful honors.

In 1975, the U.S. Olympic Committee, at the urging of its president, William Simon, changed its position and endorsed the reinstatement of Thorpe. Nevertheless, the International Olympic Committee would not budge. At last, in October 1982, after meeting with Simon, new IOC president Juan Antonio Samaranch proposed the restoration of Thorpe's amateur status. The organization's nine-member executive committee unanimously agreed, and the ban against Thorpe was lifted.

In its typically evasive manner, however, the IOC decided that Thorpe's name would be added to the record books as the 1912 pentathlon and decathlon "co-

Six of Thorpe's seven children celebrate the restoration of their father's Olympic medals at a ceremony in 1983. Juan Antonio Samaranch (center), president of the International Olympic Committee, played a key role in the reversal of a 70-year-old injustice.

champion," along with the actual second-place finishers. Despite such waffling, the sports public knew who the real gold medalist was. The IOC issued duplicate gold medals, and on January 18, 1983, Samaranch presented them to Thorpe's children. A 70-year-old injustice finally was made right.

When sports authorities selected Thorpe in 1950 as their athlete of the half-century, they made both a wise and an obvious choice. In the years since, no single sports figure has exhibited the kind of versatility that earned Thorpe that accolade. One can only hope—and indeed, expect—that in the year 2000, the sports experts of that day will do the same as their colleagues of 50 years before and name Jim Thorpe the greatest athlete of the entire 20th century.

CHRONOLOGY

1888	Born on May 28 near Bellemont in Oklahoma Territory
1898	Enrolls in the Haskell Institute
1904	Enrolls in Carlisle Indian School in Carlisle, Pennsylvania
1907	Joins the Carlisle varsity track and football teams
1909–10	On leave from Carlisle; plays minor-league baseball with Rocky Mount in the East Carolina League
1911	Named first team all-American
1912	Wins pentathlon and decathlon gold medals at Olympics in Stockholm
1913	Stripped of Olympic medals when his 1909–10 professional baseball activities are revealed; signs a three-year contract with the New York Giants baseball team
1916–20	Plays halfback and serves as head coach for the Canton Bulldogs
1922–23	Organizes, coaches, and plays for the Oorang Indians, an all-Indian pro football team
1926	Plays his last full season in the National Football League, with Canton
1929–45	Works as a laborer, movie extra, and lecturer
1945	Serves briefly in the merchant marine at the end of World War II; resumes his lecture career after the war; marries Patricia Gladys Askew
1950	Named the Greatest Football Player of the Half-Century and the Greatest Athlete of the Half-Century by two AP polls
1951	Film biography, *Jim Thorpe—All-American*, released
1953	Dies of a massive heart attack in Lomita, California, on March 28
1963	Inducted as a charter member of the Pro Football Hall of Fame in Canton, Ohio
1973	The Amateur Athletic Union reinstates Thorpe's amateur status for the period 1909–12
1982–83	The International Olympic Committee restores Thorpe's Olympic records and returns his medals to his family

FURTHER READING

Durant, John, and Les Etter. *Highlights of College Football*. New York: Hastings House, 1970.

Gobrecht, Wilbur J. *Jim Thorpe, Carlisle Indian*. Carlisle, PA: Cumberland County Historical Society, 1972.

McCallum, Jack. "The Regilding of a Legend." *Sports Illustrated* 51, no. 18 (October 25, 1982): 48–65.

Neft, David S., and Richard M. Cohen. *The Sports Encyclopedia: Pro Football, Volume 1—the Early Years (1892–1959)*. Ridgefield, CT: Sports Products, 1987.

Newcombe, Jack. *The Best of the Athletic Boys: The White Man's Impact on Jim Thorpe*. Garden City, NY: Doubleday, 1975.

Newcombe, Jack, ed. *The Fireside Book of Football*. New York: Simon & Schuster, 1964.

Sullivan, George. *The Great Running Backs*. New York: Putnam, 1972.

Wallechinsky, David. *The Complete Book of the Olympics*. Rev. ed. New York: Penguin Books, 1988.

Wheeler, Robert W. *Jim Thorpe: World's Greatest Athlete*. Norman: University of Oklahoma Press, 1983.

INDEX

PICTURE CREDITS

BOB BERNOTAS is a freelance writer living in New York City. He holds a doctorate in political theory from Johns Hopkins University and has taught philosophy and political science at Morgan State and Towson State Universities. His published works include several books on American government, numerous articles on jazz and sports, and biographies of Amiri Baraka, Sitting Bull, and Brigham Young.

W. DAVID BAIRD is the Howard A. White Professor of History at Pepperdine University in Malibu, California. He holds a Ph.D. from the University of Oklahoma and was formerly on the faculty of history at the University of Arkansas, Fayetteville, and Oklahoma State University. He has served as president of both the Western History Association, a professional organization, and Phi Alpha Theta, the international honor society for students of history. Dr. Baird is also the author of *The Quapaw Indians: A History of the Downstream People* and *Peter Pitchlynn: Chief of the Choctaws* and the editor of *A Creek Warrior of the Confederacy: The Autobiography of Chief G. W. Grayson.*